THE SILENT SINO-RUSSIAN

INVISIBLE

WAR TO BRING DOWN AMERICA

COLONEL G.L. LAMBORN
USAR RETIRED

Published by White Hart Publications,
an imprint of Our Written Lives, LLC.

Fonts and photography licensed for use.

Library of Congress Cataloging-in-Publication Data
Lamborn, G.L.
Invisible: The Sino-Russian War to Bring Down America
Library of Congress Control Number: 2022905683

Copyright ©2022 G.L. Lamborn
ISBN: 978-1-942923-55-8

DISCLAIMER

ACKNOWLEDGMENTS

I wish to acknowledge the valuable assistance I have received while writing this extended essay from December 2021 to February 2022. In a very real sense, this essay was a team effort and I am grateful for the information sent my way and for everyone's encouragement.

Chief among those I wish to thank is Dr. Arturo G. Munoz, senior RAND analyst in Washington, D.C. His encouragement of this effort was critical to its successful conclusion. Dr. Munoz pointed me to many sources of information cited in the essay.

Dr. Lisa Drozdick, a San Antonio-based psychologist, assisted me with the "Belief and Unbelief" section, and in helping me understand why certain persons form and hold irrational beliefs such as conspiracy theories.

Greatly appreciated is Oxford Professor Peter Frankopan whose work "The New Silk Roads" stimulated my interest. Anyone interested in China's Belt and Road Initiative should read his book.

Great appreciation for Washington Attorney Jim Bierman and San Francisco's Dr. Raphael Danziger, who both supplied papers and reporting relevant to this essay.

I also wish to thank the members of our informal "China Colleagues" group for sharing news items and magazine selections.

Ms. Rachael Hartman did the editing and design work required to transform my scribbling into the finished product.

This extended essay was a team effort, and I greatly appreciate everyone's help. The errors, however, are mine alone.

G.L. Lamborn
Colonel, USAR (Ret.)
San Antonio, Texas
February 2022

AUTHOR'S NOTE

This book combines a series of essays on the subject of Sino-Russian subversion which were written and officially reviewed prior to the February 24, 2022 Russian invasion of Ukraine. It does not attempt to report what is taking place today or this week. That is journalism's duty.

Rather, its purpose is to provide historical and cultural context which help explain the news of the day and the foundations of visceral Russian and Chinese hatred of the West, the United States in particular.

G.L.L.

CONTENTS

PRECIS

Opinions cannot survive if one has no chance to fight for them.
Thomas Mann[1]

The Russian Federation and the People's Republic of China have one great interest in common. Although only a dream at this time, Beijing and Moscow would like nothing better than to see America defeated, humiliated, and rendered inconsequential in world affairs. They want to see our nation weakened and our people divided.

Their means of achieving that destructive goal is to use persistent, low-visibility measures to misinform, mislead, and divide American public opinion. They aim to co-opt American industry and intellect, and to reduce confidence in our long-established Constitutional procedures.

The Chinese Communist Party pursue their dream of destroying America with patience and perseverance. Time is their greatest resource. The Chinese strategy is protracted and profound. Americans barely comprehend their theory of conflict, or their use of indirect measures against enemies.

The Russians are more direct, using active measures to divide the American people. They continue to use spies and propaganda as they did historically, but now technology aids in spreading their lies and agenda.

The following provides a historical and cultural context of the foundation of visceral Russian and Chinese hatred of the West— hatred of the United States in particular. It is important to understand the roots of Russian and Chinese hostility to explain current affairs.

---

[1] German philosopher, lived 1875-1955

For too long, the West has deluded itself into believing *"the Chinese and Russians will change and be more like us."* Perhaps centuries hence there will be liberal democracy, the rule of law, and respect for human rights in both Moscow and Beijing, but that is extremely unlikely in our lifetime. What the United States and its sister democracies must do is to take China and Russia as they are. We cannot view them as we would wish them to be. Once we accept reality, we must make appropriate defensive measures.

Both dictatorships intend ill for us, and they are conducting a silent war against us.

When bad men combine, the good must associate; else they will fall one by one, an unpitied sacrifice in a contemptible struggle.
Edmund Burke[2]

---

[2] British political philosopher, lived 1729-1797

PART ONE

TWO OLD COMRADES

CHAPTER 1

QUIET PLEASE, WAR IN PROGRESS

*Warfare is now escaping from the boundaries of bloody massacre,
and exhibiting a trend towards low casualties, or even none at all,
and yet high intensity. This is information warfare, financial warfare,
trade warfare, and other entirely new forms of war, new areas opened
up in the domain of warfare. In this sense, there is now no domain which
warfare cannot use, and there is almost no domain which does not have
warfare's offensive pattern.*[1]

Colonels Qiao Liang and Wang Xiangsui

Make no mistake, we are already at war whether we realize it or
not. The United States has been under intensive attack for at least
a decade, very likely far longer. The nature of this protracted attack
is so sophisticated the American public barely notices. Quite unlike
anything our Armed Forces would recognize as war, the attack on
America is quiet, almost imperceptible. The invisible war is like
groundwater, patiently eating away at stone until it creates a cave
and, eventually, causes the roof and walls to collapse.[2]

China's war against America has several unique aspects. First,
it is a war in which China is making use of the physical and
intellectual resources of its main enemy, the United States. The
Chinese have "lured in deep"[3] American corporations to assist its
People's Liberation Army to achieve technological parity with U.S.
Armed Forces. Thousands of Chinese students, especially those at

---

[1] Qiao Liang and Wang Xiangsui, Unrestricted Warfare, p. 189

[2] Chinese saying: "Water is the softest of all things, but with time and perseverance it can wear away the hardest stone." The Chinese are renowned for their patience and perseverance. We are the hard stone.

[3] "Luring in deep" was official PLA doctrine in the 1950s to 1970s. It posited encouraging a foreign enemy (Russia or the U.S.) to invade deeply before becoming overextended and overwhelmed by China. Used here, it signifies luring in foreign (mainly U.S.) corporations which are then made to serve China's interests.

the graduate level, bring home immense amounts of advanced U.S. research, knowledge, and even samples. Loss of U.S. technology is calculated to be in the billions of dollars.

Second, China's war against America is a struggle in which the Chinese intend to *avoid*, if possible, the use of military force. They would rather achieve victory indirectly by separating America from its allies, isolating the U.S. from the global community, and expanding China's influence through its "Belt and Road Initiative," aggressive diplomacy, and rapidly growing financial and technological power.

A third unique aspect of the war against America is that, with the help of its Russian ally, China is quietly developing capabilities to interfere with America's infrastructure. Russia has already shown its ability to paralyze a part of the American infrastructure by shutting down the Colonial Pipeline. Both China and Russia aim to have the same power over America.

In the fourth aspect, Beijing intends to defeat the United States by encouraging social and political unrest inside America—also with Moscow's help. China's ultimate strategy aims at bringing about the collapse of the United States from within. The aim is achieved by causing thousands of Americans to reject and disparage American political and social institutions. By creating or encouraging conflict inside the United States, the Russians and Chinese intend to paralyze America at home and abroad.

How can this be? China, and its ally, Russia, base their strategies on a careful appraisal of America's strengths and weaknesses as they perceive them.

Americans communicate. Perhaps more than any other people on Earth, Americans seem addicted to news and social media, and communicate almost continually with each other.

American industry, including banking and commerce, is highly dependent upon Internet linkage and advanced data communication networks.

Americans travel daily. Millions depend upon predictable railroad, aircraft, or mass transit schedules for their livelihoods and businesses.

American utilities, including generating facilities, well heads, power transmission lines, oil and gas pipelines, and refineries provide the nation's reliable energy.

American farmers, the most efficient in the world, are capable of feeding the nation, but only if they have reliable access to financing, transportation, and markets.

America is an open Constitutional society which prides itself on the uncensored flow of public and private information. Political and social institutions are dependent upon freedom of expression and *toleration of diverse political and social opinions.*

Our Chinese adversaries and their Russian associates are well aware of these realities. They also are aware that any one of these aspects of the American economy and our open political structure can be disrupted with surprising ease.

Beijing and Moscow believe that in order to secure their own authoritarian political systems it is necessary to degrade or destroy ours. In part, their aim is shaped by ideological imperatives. Of even greater importance, the Sino-Russian desire to bring down the United States derives from their expansionist policies as Great Powers who see America as an obstacle to achieving their goals. Each country has fairly obvious territorial, economic, and political goals.

The struggle between our open, democratic system and their closed, authoritarian systems is very much one-sided. Russian and Chinese operatives have relatively easy access to American targets. In contrast, Vladimir Putin has returned Russia to that country's traditional limitations on people's rights and has re-installed extensive government control over information and the state-directed economy. Arrest or elimination of democratic political opposition remains a key element in how the Russian Federation is ruled. The CPSU may be gone, but the legacy of centuries-old autocracy lingers on.[4]

China's level of political control goes well beyond that of Russia. Under the Chinese Communist Party, China is a totalitarian country in which the Party has the tightest possible control over every

---

[4] Russia can fairly be said to have had only two "relatively democratic" periods in its entire history – that of Alexander Kerensky in 1917 and the brief period under Boris Yeltsin in the 1990s.

citizen. Indeed, China's nationwide surveillance system comes very close to resembling that described decades ago by British novelist George Orwell. In his book, "We Have Been Harmonized," German journalist Kai Strittmatter, who lived in China for twenty years, described the omnipresent surveillance capabilities of the Public Security Bureau and local police. The police and PSB are able to monitor people's most intimate daily activities. Very strict controls are in place over the urban populace thanks to the technological prowess of Huawei and ZTE.[5]

In addition, the Chinese have erected what has been dubbed the "Great Firewall." Only Party-approved information can leave China, and only Party-approved outside information can ever reach the average Chinese citizen. Very little objective information from the West penetrates the Orwellian shadow-land. Inside China itself, very little objective information about national policymaking reaches the average Chinese citizen. The Party keeps a close hold on all available information.

In general, the American public knows relatively little about China or Russia, their histories and current political structures, or their national goals. It is this ignorance, combined with the characteristic vulnerabilities of open networked American society, which gives the leaders of closed states an operational advantage in penetrating and manipulating our politics, economy, social structure, and aspects of our culture.[6]

In its 2019 report on foreign interference in the American elections of 2016 and 2018, the Department of Homeland Security (DHS) noted, ". . . foreign influence and disinformation should be seen as a continuous, ongoing assault on the United States, rather than [as] a series of discrete, targeted, event-specific campaigns."[7] Political influence is merely one facet of the relentless drive to weaken and eventually destroy the United States.

---

[5] Kai Strittmatter, We Have Been Harmonized, 2019.

[6] Kendall-Taylor, Andrea, and David Shullman. "How Russia and China Undermine Democracy," Foreign Affairs, 2 October 2018. www.foreignaffairs.com/articles/china/2018-10-02/how-russia-and-china-underminedemocracy.

[7] Department of Homeland Security (DHS), "Interim Report of the Countering Foreign Influence Subcommittee, 21 May 2019; pp. 17-18.

A case in point is the May 2021 shut-down of the Colonial Pipeline, which deprived many eastern states of fuel for several weeks. The Colonial Pipeline provides 45% of gasoline, oil, and jet fuel to the southeastern U.S. The pipeline company, headquartered outside of Atlanta, reportedly transports more than 100 million gallons of various fuels each day from Texas to the East Coast.[8] Closure of the Colonial Pipeline as a result of a Russian ransomware attack not only inconvenienced tens of thousands of motorists, but threatened the shutdown of inter-city trucking, airline operations, and military functions at bases from Virginia to Georgia.

The ransomware attack was ostensibly carried out by an independent band of hackers in Russia who supposedly desired only payment of a ransom.[9] It is simply inconceivable that in an authoritarian state like the Russian Federation, an "independent" group of hackers could operate under the noses of Russia's highly effective security service, the FSB.[10] Only an extremely naïve person could accept the story that Vladimir Putin and his government had no knowledge whatsoever of this talented group of Internet brigands. A more likely explanation of the shutdown is that it was a Russian test of America's infrastructure and cyber defenses hidden under a fig leaf of plausible deniability.

It must be stated plainly that far from the "rogue group" Russia's cover story would have us believe, the attack was carried out with the approval, and very likely, at the explicit direction of the highest levels of the Russian government. It proved to be a successful probe of American vulnerability, and it will not be the last of such probes.

For its part, China uses all means at its disposal to steal American technology, research materials, and business strategies. In 2015, computer experts at Amazon noticed some anomalies in servers they had purchased from a San Francisco company which had subcontracted to the notorious Huawei Corporation of Shanghai.

---

[8] Information taken from the Colonial Pipeline company's website.

[9] The hackers were paid the equivalent of $4.4 million in Bitcoin. A month later about $2.3 million was recovered.

[10] The Federativnye Sluzhba Bezopasnosti = Federal Security Service, the lineal descendent of the KGB's Second Chief Directorate – is tasked with internal security and suppression of all political opposition.

Rightly concerned, Amazon quietly brought its findings to the attention of U.S. officials. Upon close inspection of the motherboards in the Huawei-modified servers, they found a microchip that was not part of the original design. The microchip was a tiny back door enabling the PRC intelligence service unauthorized access to the information on the servers.[11]

The significance of Huawei's technical modification of the servers was two-fold. Its primary function was to enable Chinese technical espionage. Any information stored on a modified server was automatically compromised to a listener in China's Ministry of State Security. A second benefit was to enable Chinese technical operations officers[12] the option of deleting or altering any of the information on the server. From the perspective of the Chinese intelligence service, such technical theft or modification would go unnoticed and therefore be completely deniable.

The problem at hand for the U.S. Government was the fact that the Defense Department, U.S. Navy, and dozens of corporations used the Huawei-modified servers. Indeed, according to press reports, 7,000 of those servers were put in service with corporations in New York, Singapore, Amsterdam, Hong Kong, Tokyo, San Jose, and other cities.[13]

A third means of hurting American interests is through classical spy operations. In addition to Russian and Chinese efforts to penetrate American policymaking and intelligence circles, the Chinese give special attention to economic targets.

A case in point is that of Tan Hongjin, a young CalTech Ph.D. who was employed by the Phillips 66 Corporation in Bartlesville, Oklahoma. During his stay with Phillips, Tan illegally downloaded dozens of company proprietary files which he passed to a Chinese intelligence officer. Phillips and the Department of Justice assessed the value of the stolen technical data at $1 billion. Tan was arrested by the FBI, convicted of espionage, and sentenced to three years

---

[11] Jordan Robinson and Michael Riley, "The Big Hack: How China Used a Tiny Chip to Infiltrate U.S. Companies," Bloomberg Businessweek, 4 October 2018.

[12] A technical operations officer is known in the trade as a "TOPS officer" for "tech-ops."

[13] Robinson and Riley, op.cit.

in prison and a $150,000 fine. According to a press report, Tan has been offered a job in China upon his release from prison.[14]

In his testimony before Congress, Bill Priestap, the head of the FBI's counterintelligence division, stated: "*The Chinese government is attempting to acquire or steal not only the plans and intentions of the United States government, but also the ideas and innovations of the very people that make our economy so incredibly successful.*"[15]

Oxford professor Peter Frankopan estimates that Chinese theft of American intellectual property inflicts losses of a minimum of $225 billion *per year* and possibly much more.[16]

These concerns are magnified by large-scale theft of intellectual property (IP) by China and others, which one influential report claimed came at a cost of some $225-$600 billion per year to the U.S. economy. According to a different study, Chinese cyber attacks have focused on "massive theft of information and intellectual property to increase China's economic competitiveness and accelerate its efforts to dominate world markets in key advanced technologies."[17]

The point being made is that by using traditional espionage and the latest computer technology, our adversaries have demonstrated their capability and willingness to steal sensitive information, compromise or alter databases, and paralyze critical parts of our economy. Their interests run the full gamut—not merely political subversion, but acquisition of sensitive American technology and theft of economic secrets. As noted, this activity is not sporadic or occasional, but relentless.

---

[14] Energy Review, "Chinese employee charged with stealing US energy secrets," 26 December 2018

[15] Energy Review, Ibid.

[16] Peter Frankopan, The New Silk Roads, p.108. Frankopan cites the Commission on the Theft of American Intellectual Property, "Update to the IP Commission Report. The Theft of American Intellectual Property: Reassessments of the Challenge and United States Policy," February 2017, and Robert Sutter, "China-Russia Relations: Strategic Implications and US Policy Options," National Bureau of Asian Research, September 2018.

[17] Ibid. p. 108

A COMMON ENEMY

The Chinese and the Russians appear to have patched up military differences dating from their border clashes in the late 1960's[18] to form a working partnership, if not a formal alliance. In connection with the Vostok-18 military exercises held in Russia, Beijing's Minister of Defense, General Wei Fenghe, paid an official visit to Moscow to affirm China's ever-closer relationship with Russia. General Wei made the following statement for the record:

> I am visiting Russia . . . to show the world a high level of development of our bilateral relations and [the] firm determination of our armed forces to strengthen strategic cooperation. . . . The Chinese side has come to Moscow to show [the] Americans the close ties between the armed forces of Russia and China. . . . We have come to support you.[19]

Ten months earlier, Vladimir Putin and Xi Jinping released a joint statement to the effect that China and Russia were "*each other's most trustworthy strategic partners.*"[20] Putin and Xi appear to have renewed their vows again at the February 2022 Winter Olympic Games.

The foregoing pronouncement should be taken with a grain of salt. The Department of Homeland Security makes the point clear that although both the Russians and the Chinese have America as their common target, they do not necessarily move in lockstep on the same issues or even with quite the same goals in mind.

It must be noted that no two state actors have exactly the same objectives when they devise disinformation campaigns. For example, the known Chinese disinformation campaigns in the United States

---

[18] Especially the 1969 clashes over control of Ch'en-pao Island aka Damanskiy Island in Manchuria.

[19] Frankopan, op.cit.. pp. 180-2. "China's defense chief calls his Moscow trip a signal to the US," Associated Press, 3 April 2018. Vostok-18 also had contingents from both India and Pakistan.

[20] 3 July 2017; China Daily, CNBC, many other sources.

have focused on pro-Chinese propaganda and strategic economic policy, whereas known Russian campaigns focused on political discourse and election infrastructure.[21]

The foregoing observation made by Brookings analyst Alina Polyakova, while quite true, should be taken in the context of the interests and foreign policies of Russia and China. Those policies are congruent to a point, but only to a point. In at least one important way, their interests coincide—namely, their open agreement to work against the United States and Western democracies. Due to diverging perceptions of their national needs, China and Russia focus on different parts of their common target. Achieving technological superiority and financial power are of great interest to Beijing; whereas manipulating American internal political affairs—and indirectly, U.S. foreign policy—is Russia's focus.

Russia has made a habit of meddling with U.S. presidential elections since the 1964 Goldwater-Johnson contest. Russian influence in the 2016 election was nothing new. From a Russian perspective, all U.S. presidents are adversaries, but some are less objectionable than others. Moscow's goal is to provide quiet help to presidential candidates assessed as more pliable and less resistant to Russia's national interests.

This having been said, Beijing and Moscow perceive a steady polarization of American society and politics. While much of this polarization is homegrown in America—namely, between ethnic groups, political parties, and the rich and poor—Russian and Chinese entities have encouraged and even fostered the divisions. A case in point is the extremist group QAnon, which Russia cultivated from 2017 to late 2020, and with which China appears to have taken the lead since early 2021.

Since 2016, homegrown fanatics—Americans who, in effect, collaborate with foreign adversaries—have conducted an unremitting attack on American core values, including our Constitutional processes. The object of this campaign is to undermine public confidence in our democratic system and encourage enmity between groups, and distrust of our elected leaders. This destructive behavior is welcomed in Moscow and Beijing as it serves to advance their interests.

Beijing has even turned the catastrophe of the COVID-19 pandemic to its advantage. Although the virus first appeared in Wuhan, China, the Chinese foreign ministry claimed COVID-19 originated in U.S. Army laboratories and was smuggled into China.[22] Moreover, Beijing spreads the word that America piggishly withholds vaccines from Third World countries, but that China generously shares its vaccines with all who need them.

What the foregoing makes clear is that the United States is under attack. True, it is a quiet, subtle attack, but we are under attack just the same—from many directions and in many ways. As Colonels Qiao and Wang observed, *"There is now no domain which warfare cannot use, and there is almost no domain which does not have warfare's offensive pattern."*

Russia and China would like nothing better than to see the United States humiliated and put down, degraded and dishonored, fatally weakened, and ultimately rendered of no consequence in a world which thereafter is theirs to shape as they please.

Of the two countries, China is by far the more dangerous. It is more sophisticated, has a much broader and more fully developed doctrinal approach to war, and vastly more resources, both human and material. China certainly is prepared for a short, intensive war of the kind familiar to The Pentagon, but it much prefers to conduct a protracted struggle over years and decades using a far broader range of "weapons that are not weapons" until its principal adversary—America—is exhausted, bankrupted, and brought under China's economic and political control.

The United States customarily prepares only for high-tech military wars in which the American public plays little or no part. The public at large has little interest in foreign affairs and are merely spectators watching the evening news. The Defense Department rightly considers China its primary adversary, but seems to be preparing

---

[22] Zhao Lijian, Ministry of Foreign Affairs, Twitter post [@zlj517] 12 March 2020

for exactly the wrong kind of struggle.[23] Figuratively, Washington is using hardware and technology which Beijing can easily match. After all, Corporate America, with the help of U.S. universities, has furnished China with much of its weapons technology. Beijing, however, is capable of orchestrating not merely ships and soldiers, but "fourth dimension" means of ensnaring and ultimately defeating America. And that is its plan.

What must be understood clearly is that the Chinese concept of conflict, and the exertion of its national power, fundamentally differs from the traditional western view which we hold. The Clausewitzian view takes note of state and society only as adjuncts of military power.[24] By contrast, the Chinese take into consideration the totality of their adversary. They include appraisal of strengths and weaknesses in social and educational levels, cultural norms, ethnic identity and conflicts, demographic factors, class conflicts, and the strength of a national identity among the people. They look at religious concerns, and even at things such as medicine, the arts, and sports.

The Chinese view is total; it is infinitely broader than our own. Americans would do well to study the Chinese view of the quiet war in which we are engaged, and to adjust our actions and thinking in such a way as to defeat our enemies' strategies.

All warfare is based on deception. Therefore, when capable, feign incapacity; when active, inactivity. When near, make it appear that you are far away; when far away, that you are near.[25]

Sun Tzu

---

[23] See Hal Brands and Michael Beckley, "Washington is Preparing for the Wrong War With China," Foreign Affairs, 16 December 2021. Author concurs with the writers' view that "military" conflict with China is a "wrong war," but believes China's concept of "conflict" is far broader than anything The Pentagon or U.S. Government envisions.

[24] The Jominian view, held by nearly all Air Force and Naval officers, and even some ground forces officers, is highly mathematical, weapons-oriented, and places little, if any, importance on political, social or psychological factors.

[25] Sun Tzu as quoted in S.B. Griffith (trans) The Art of War, p. 66

CHAPTER 2

CHINA'S CONCEPT OF PROTRACTED WAR

Accordingly, having made an objective and comprehensive appraisal of all the circumstances concerning both the enemy and ourselves, we point out that the only way to final victory is the strategy of protracted war, and we reject the groundless theory of quick victory. We maintain that we must strive to secure all the conditions indispensable to final victory, and the more fully and the earlier these conditions are secured, the surer we shall be of victory and the earlier we shall win it.[1]

Mao Tsetung

China has the most ancient, and possibly the most profound, tradition of political-military thinking of any country. Their classic treatise on military strategy is the *Sun Tzu Bing-fa* (the *"Soldier's Method of Master Sun"*). The manual dates from the late Warring States period of the 5th century BCE and has been studied and commented upon by two millennia of Chinese generals.

The Soldier's Method laid down the basic Chinese doctrine that still guides their military thinking. Two brilliant Chinese strategists, both senior PLA officers, closely mirror Sun Tzu's guidance. While their theoretical work examines campaigns conducted by the United States and its allies in the late 20th century, they quote Sun Tzu frequently in their 1999 book, *Unrestricted Warfare*. It is important that we take a look at some of the cardinal principles taught more than two thousand years ago, since they are still relevant today.

Unlike Western strategists such as Clausewitz or Jomini, Sun Tzu advocated attaining victory with minimal fighting, ideally with no fighting at all. His most famous axiom is:

---

[1] On Protracted War (1938), in Selected Military Writings of Mao Tse-tung, pp. 207-208

For to win one hundred victories in one hundred battles is not the acme of skill. To subdue the enemy without fighting is the acme of skill. Thus, what is of supreme importance in war is to attack the enemy's strategy.[2]

China aims at gradually surrounding an enemy using time and patience as elements of strategy, steadily eroding an enemy's ability and willingness to resist. The Chinese use political and psychological measures to internally disrupt their adversaries. In keeping with Master Sun's guidance, the objective is not necessarily to destroy an enemy in battle, but to compel him to accept one's will and eventually absorb him.

Toward that end, Sun Tzu and generations of Chinese commanders held that extensive measures must be taken to soften up a target or potential adversary well before the onset of overt hostilities. Among these measures are moves to dissolve the enemy's alliances, demoralize his soldiers, and sow confusion and doubt among the enemy state's ministers and people.[3] In sum, the ideal would be to weaken an adversary to the point at which his defeat will be certain if continued by battle, making the use of force unnecessary to subdue the enemy.[4]

Drawing upon the ancient wisdom of Master Sun, his contemporary disciples, PLA Colonels Qiao Liang and Wang Xiangsui, have laid out the following as doctrine for China's armed forces:

However, by using the combination method, a completely different scenario and game can occur: if the attacking side secretly musters large amounts of capital without the enemy nation being aware of this at all and launches a sneak attack against its financial markets, then after causing a financial crisis, buries a computer virus and

---

[2] Sun Tzu as quoted in S.B. Griffith (trans) The Art of War, p. 77

[3] Sun Tzu, op.cit.

[4] A view also held by British strategist, B.H.Liddell-Hart. See his work Strategy, pp. 338-339

hacker detachment in the opponent's computer system in advance, while at the same time carrying out a network attack against the enemy so that the civilian electricity network, traffic dispatching network, financial transaction network, telephone communications network, and mass media network are completely paralyzed, this will cause the enemy nation to fall into social panic, street riots, and a political crisis. There is finally the forceful bearing down by the army, and military means are utilized in gradual stages until the enemy is forced to sign a dishonorable peace treaty. This admittedly does not attain to the domain spoken of by Sun Tzu, wherein "the other army is subdued without fighting." However, it can be considered to be "subduing the other army through clever operations." It is very clear who was superior and who inferior when comparing these two methods of operation.[5]

The Chinese are known for their patience and ability to take "the long view." Seldom are the Chinese in a great rush to attain some objective.

A BATTLEFIELD BEYOND THE BATTLEFIELD

The new, expanded view of Chinese doctrine far transcends the narrower Western, particularly American, view of war. The Chinese have developed a fully integrated doctrine that envisions eroding an enemy's civilian as well as military capability, and suppressing an enemy's willingness to resist political demands. The aim, according to Qiao and Wang, is to paralyze civil society and bring about the defeat of an enemy's armed forces from within. In their words:

Whether it involves electromagnetic energy weapons for hard destruction or soft-strikes by computer logic bombs, network viruses, or media weapons, all are focused on

---

[5] Qiao and Wang, op.cit.; pp. 145-146

paralyzing and undermining [an enemy,] not personnel casualties.[6]

In the event of an outbreak of armed hostilities, paralyzing the American command and control system remains the uppermost objective. The second objective would be the compromise of transportation and communication systems. Added to this would be disruption of banking, electric power, and water systems. Qiao and Wang envision a "battlefield beyond the battlefield" which would touch every corner of the non-military areas of an adversary. In their appraisal of American society, which the Chinese openly consider decadent and in rapid decline, they place great emphasis on exacerbating social divisions to speed American collapse. What distinguishes Chinese doctrine from our own is its focus on creating chaos in the civilian "rear area," which is intended to hamper the functioning of civil government.

Echoing thoughts from American futurist Alvin Toffler, Colonels Qiao and Wang state:

> Today's wars will affect the price of gasoline in pipelines, the price of food in supermarkets, and the price of securities on the stock exchange. They will also disrupt the ecological balance, and push their way into every one of our homes by way of the television screen. . . . The war will be fought and won in a war beyond the battlefield; the struggle for victory will take place on a battlefield beyond the battlefield.[7]

Where is this "battlefield beyond the battlefield" of which they speak? This battlefield is in the local streets, neighborhoods, and living rooms of America. It is in the minds of the American people. With the help of their Russian associates, the Chinese military and secret services are quite prepared to bring the war directly to the American people. In fact, they are doing so even now.

---

[6] Qiao Liang and Wang Xiangsui, Unrestricted Warfare, 1999, p. 29

[7] Qiao and Wang, op.cit, p. 179

This invisible war has three parts, and all are fully integrated. The first part would be a concerted effort to shut down as many vital services as possible. The closure of the Colonial Pipeline by the Russians is an example of what is possible. The near collapse of the electric power system in Texas during Winter Storm Uri in early 2021 was brought about by a combination of bad weather, corporate greed, and political ineptitude. In the event of armed conflict, bad weather will not be needed to bring down power systems, as they are linked and run by computers vulnerable to hacking.

As mentioned by Colonels Qiao and Wang, a team of skilled hackers is all that is required to bring down any utility in America. Whether that hacker team happens to be Russian or Chinese matters very little.

Banks and brokerage houses also are dependent upon computer networks. As noted by Qiao and Wang, a platoon of trolls assisted by an army of bots could paralyze the American financial system. With no ability to deposit, withdraw, or transfer funds, millions of Americans would be unable to make payments or purchase necessities. For a day or two, financial paralysis would be an inconvenience. For an extended period of even a few weeks, such a blow would cause major economic damage.

Let us imagine the reaction if a mere fifty million Americans in America's top seven cities suddenly found their credit cards invalidated and unable to function. The result would not only be economic chaos, but very likely panic. The banks and credit houses would obviously do their best to reconstitute all the hacked accounts, but the impact of a massive credit hack of this nature would leave commuters stranded, families unable to buy food, customers unable to pay for goods, ATMS useless, and many other essential services unavailable.

America's banking and financial system is a prime target. Qiao and Wang go into some detail about how an attacker might secretly muster large amounts of capital to doom an adversary. The American dollar might be a tempting target for Beijing and its banks.

Modern currencies rest on the full faith and credit of the issuing government or central bank to maintain and redeem their currency at face value. Should doubts arise about the stability of a certain currency, it can be subjected to attack, precisely as George Soros attacked the British pound in 1992. By shorting the British pound, Soros pocketed the equivalent of $1 billion U.S. dollars.[8] His move forced the British government to withdraw from a European currency arrangement and devalue the pound.

It is no secret that China holds immense quantities of U.S. debt, both public and private. China is a creditor nation thanks to America's profligate spending on Chinese goods of every type. At any moment, China could place its Treasury Notes and other holdings, which amount to several trillion dollars, on the global market. The result of such a move could be severe buffeting of the U.S. dollar, and perhaps lead to devaluation. China might then offer its "more stable" Renminbi—the Yuan—as a replacement for the dollar as the World Reserve Currency. Having the world's goods and services denominated in RMB rather than USD would give Beijing immense economic power over global trade.

Disruption of electrical, pipeline and financial systems would hamstring airline operations, commercial trucking, mining and manufacturing, a host of other essential activities, and would create social panic. Adding to social chaos, the Chinese would call forth violence-prone treasonous thugs like QAnon and groups dedicated to violent radicalism. Qiao and Wang explicitly refer to street riots that result in social panic.

Sardonically, Colonels Qiao and Wang refer to a young People's Liberation Army trooper's inquiry on the location of the battlefield.

Thus, the battlefield is omnipresent. Just think, if it's even possible to start a war in a computer room or a stock exchange that will send an enemy country to its doom, then is there non-battlespace anywhere? If that young lad

---

[8] See Investopedia, "How Did George Soros Break the Bank of England?" Soros is mentioned (unfavorably) in Qiao and Wang's work, *Unrestricted Warfare.* The point being made here is that a Central Bank such as the Bank of China is capable of inflicting far more damage on a currency than is an individual investor, even one as wealthy as Soros.

setting out with his orders should ask today: 'Where is the battlefield?' the answer would be: 'Everywhere.'[9]

It is clear that China's evolving doctrine encompasses dimensions of conflict ranging from nuclear weapons to the armchairs of Americans who wish to think of themselves as non-combatants. For theorists like Colonels Qiao and Wang there is no such thing as non-battlespace. From their perspective, organized armed forces as understood by The Pentagon are nearly irrelevant. The Chinese expect enormous domestic pressure exerted on the American political system to be so great it compels top leadership to sue for an armistice, and would require the U.S. Armed Forces to stand down. As the colonels note: " . . . *in the information age, the influence exerted by a nuclear bomb is perhaps less than the influence exerted by a hacker.*"[10]

Throughout their book, *Unrestricted Warfare*, Colonels Qiao and Wang repeatedly note America's apparently blind fixation on weaponry—such as "smart missiles" or F-35 aircraft—as being the absolute and only answer to supremacy on a battlefield. They make a compelling case that most senior American generals, and even the majority of civilian strategists, pay too much attention to equipment and technology, but almost no attention to the object of war. In the colonels' view, American strategic thinking lags very far behind an expanded concept of what the battlefield is, and where it is.

As Master Sun noted 2,500 years ago, "*Thus a victorious army wins its victories before seeking battle; an army destined to defeat fights [only] in the hope of winning.*"[11]

SUN TZU'S CHAPTER THIRTEEN

Many places in his book *Soldier's Method*, Sun Tzu notes the importance of "knowing oneself and knowing one's enemy." His advice is to know both very well, but with the caveat that all war is based upon deception of one's adversary. Toward that end, Sun Tzu's

[9] Qiao and Wang, op.cit., p. 43

[10] Qiao and Wang, op.cit,, p. 47

[11] Sun Tzu as quoted in S.B. Griffith (trans) The Art of War, p. 87

admonition is to conduct vigorous and extensive campaigns, not merely of espionage, but of disinformation well before the onset of armed conflict. It is necessary to use resources advantageously and, to the extent possible, employ the human resources of one's adversary.

The thirteenth and final chapter of *Soldier's Method* lays out Sun Tzu's thinking on the subjects of intelligence collection and deception. Both are matters of great importance to him. He identifies five categorizes of agents, or spies, and their uses. One of these five categories is the expendable agent who is sent to foreign states to provide false information and intentionally mislead its leaders and people.

Master Sun states their role simply and directly: "*Expendable agents are those of our own spies who are deliberately given fabricated information.*"[12] Put directly, their purpose is to mislead and misdirect an enemy, causing him to make serious mistakes in his planning.[13]

One of Sun's commentators, the ninth century T'ang dynasty general and historian Tu Yu,[14] elaborated on the Master's terse statement as follows:

> We leak information which is actually false and allow our own agents to learn it. When these agents operating in enemy territory are taken [ed. captured] by him they are certain to report this false information. The enemy will believe it and make preparations accordingly. But our actions will of course not accord with this, and the enemy will put the spies to death.[15]

The fourteenth century Ming dynasty commentator, General Chang Yu, added to understanding the use of expendable agents in these words:

---

[12] Sun Tzu as quoted in S.B. Griffith (trans) The Art of War, p. 146

[13] Napoleon once quipped, "Never interrupt an enemy when he is making a mistake."

[14] The T'ang dynasty, one of China's most creative and glorious dynasties, lasted from 618 to 907 CE. Tu Yu, a member of a family with generations of official service, lived from 735 to 812 CE.

[15] Sun Tzu as quoted in S.B. Griffith (trans) The Art of War, p. 146

It is because doubled agents know in what respects the enemy can be deceived that expendable agents may be sent to convey false information. This is because the doubled agent knows those of his countrymen who are covetous as well as those officials who have been remiss in office. These we can tempt into our service.[16]

All foreign intelligence services are constantly in search of individuals with inclinations or vulnerabilities that render them susceptible to recruitment. Recruitment places such individuals under control and at the direction of the recruiting intelligence service's case officers. These double-agent collaborators, witting or unwitting, also serve the same end. The idea of penetrating an adversary through operational use of a regime's own officials and citizens goes back millennia. In the commentary added to *Soldier's Method*, a reference is made to the destruction from within of the ancient Hsia and Shang dynasties.[17]

Tu Mu, a poet and general of the T'ang dynasty, elaborated on Master Sun's mention of native agents as being those of the enemy's country employed as spies. Tu Mu goes on at length about the various types of people in the enemy's state who could be recruited, but he concludes his listing with this observation:

Then you may rely on them to seek out the real facts of the situation in their country, and to ascertain its plans directed against you. They can as well create cleavages between the sovereign and his ministers so that these are not in harmonious accord.[18]

Today's Chinese military thinkers, though not as explicit as their T'ang and Ming predecessors, refer indirectly to the need to

---

[16] Sun Tzu as quoted in S.B. Griffith (trans) The Art of War, p. 148-149

[17] The Hsia and Shang are very ancient dynasties, overthrown due to their loss of popular support and internal treachery.

[18] Sun Tzu, op.cit., p. 145; italics added for emphasis

develop PLA espionage and disinformation capabilities among China's adversaries. It is a sad but unpleasant truth that traitors and collaborators, as well as "useful fools" such as political extremists, are found in American society. The Chinese can use these people to intensify and exploit existing political and social divisions in the U.S. The intent is to weaken China's perceived national enemy, the United States, to such a degree that it becomes unable to resist Chinese Communist political demands.

Without referring to the United States by name, Colonels Qiao and Wang state the following:

> [A] second category is the new sources of future conflicts: nationalism (racism) in declining nations; conflicts in cultural [and] religious beliefs; the spread of lethal light weapons; disputes over petroleum, fishing, and water resources; the tide of refugees and population flows; ecological disasters; and terrorism.[19]

Each of these controversial political-social issues affecting America is of operational interest to the Chinese People's Liberation Army. Any weaknesses within the country can result in turbulence in U.S. cities, and even strikes or rioting in Washington, D.C. In a time of war, such rioting or massive disturbances could prove fatal for the United States.

It is unclear whether The Pentagon fully appreciates the link between domestic political and social issues—especially widespread disturbances—and their potential for disrupting U.S. military operations. Does The Pentagon truly understand the Chinese overall strategy? Colonels Qiao and Wang, make a clear connection:

> The only difference is that in the predictable future, military operations will never again be the entire war; rather they are one dimension within the total dimension. Even adding "non-combat military operations"

---

[19] Qiao and Wang, op.cit., p. 123

as proposed by General Franks cannot count as total dimensionality. Only by adding all "non-military combat operations" aside from military operations can total dimensional war's complete significance be realized.[20]

In a word, all of the new warfare methods and strategic measures which can be provided by all of the new technology may be utilized by these fanatics to carry out all forms of financial attacks, network attacks, media attacks, or terrorist attacks. Most of these attacks are not military actions, and yet they can be completely viewed as, or equal to, warfare actions which force other nations to satisfy their own interests and demands.[21]

Although it is unclear what Qiao and Wang meant by the phrase "these fanatics," the colonels clearly advocate stirring up as much trouble as possible behind enemy lines to hamstring conventional military operations. We must be mindful of the observation made by Cypriot General George Grivas: *"My own military career has taught me that the collapse of the front usually begins from the rear."*[22]

Echoing Master Sun and many Chinese generals who commented on his *Soldier's Method* over the centuries, arguably two of China's top strategists and military thinkers, Colonels Qiao and Wang, argue that the war should be over and won, well before the first shot is fired in anger. *The war will be won in the enemy's rear area, not at the front.*

Only by avoiding frontal collisions, will it be possible for your sword to cut apart things without being damaged. This is the most basic grammar of victory for the ancient article of war.[23]

Colonels Qiao Liang and Wang Xiangsui

---

[20] Qiao Liang and Wang Xiangsui, Unrestricted Warfare, 1999, p. 102

[21] Ibid., p. 117

[22] George Grivas, General Grivas on Guerrilla Warfare, p. 11

[23] Qiao Liang and Wang Xiangsui, op.cit., p. 165

CHAPTER 3

THE RUSSIAN CONNECTION

The only secure border is one with a Russian army on both sides of it.

Russian saying

An army cannot be built without repression. The commander will always find it necessary to place the soldier between the possibility that death lies ahead and the certainty that it lies behind.[1]

Leon Trotsky

Russia has a recorded history of just over a thousand years, far shorter than its ally, China. The Christianization of Russia began with the conversion of St. Vladimir in 988 AD. The Patriarch in Constantinople sanctioned Vladimir's baptism, and the infant Russian state was tied to Eastern Orthodoxy rather than the Roman rites practiced in Poland, Hungary, or the lands of Western Europe. Its alphabet, Cyrillic, designed by two Eastern Orthodox priests, further distanced the land from its western neighbors. Because of its geography and weight of history, Russia produced massive armies and excellent soldiers, but it never had a profound thinker of Sun Tzu's stature.[2]

Early Russia was a product of a fusion of the existing Slavic population with Scandinavian Vikings, known as the Varangians, who made use of Russia's rivers to trade with the Byzantine Empire. The rivers provided the only viable north-south means of transiting the vast steppe lands of the Russian plain, which extended from the Carpathians to the Urals. The people living along the Dnepr

---

[1] Leon Trotsky, founder of the Red Army

[2] Both Carl von Clausewitz and Antoine Jomini served in Russian uniform – Prussian-born Clausewitz during the Napoleonic wars and Swiss-born Jomini until his death in 1868.

became known as the Rus. Kiev was the original center of the first Russian state.

Unfortunately for Kievan Rus, geography played its fatal card. The rivers connected the Baltic with the Black Sea and Constantinople, but the vast steppe was completely open to mounted nomadic invaders from the east. These included waves of marauders such as the Khazars, Pechenegs, and Polovtsi. Kievan Rus was doomed to extinction by an invader more powerful than any other—the Mongol Golden Horde under Batu, Jenghiz Khan's nephew. Moscow was captured and burned in the winter of 1237, and Kiev was destroyed in 1240. For 250 years, the Russians languished under Mongol rule. Any ties they had developed with Western European kingdoms or Byzantium were severed.

When Russia began to assert itself after the expulsion of the Mongols in 1480, the lesson for the newly independent princes of Muscovy was that security was found only in large, powerful armies. If a reminder of this truism was needed, the Polish invasion and capture of Moscow in 1609 provided it. Thereafter, Russia developed and maintained very large armies, certainly among the largest in the world. After Peter the Great's reforms, the Russian Army could take on even its most advanced European adversaries, Sweden, Prussia and France. Peter's defeat of Sweden in the Great Northern War gave Russia a window to Europe and brought it into the European state system.

It is the fate of Russia to be a vast, sprawling land of marshes, steppe, and woodlands, with no natural barriers against enemies that compelled it to become a militarized state. Peter the Great merely took reality as he found it. He attempted to graft elements of Western military technology, especially artillery, on what really was a massive, shambling peasant army. In a sense, that army remained much as it had been since its formation in the wake of the Golden Horde. It was an Asiatic army with Europeanized officers.

Asiatic or not, the Russian Army played a significant role in all major European wars of the 18th and 19th centuries, save the Franco-Prussian War of 1870. The Russian army's defeat of Napoleon in 1812 and the Congress of Vienna marked the true entry of Russia on the world stage as a Great Power. The point being made is that for centuries Russia's relative security from marauders from the east or invading armies from Europe rested on its massive armies. It still does. In the last two hundred years, Russia's acceptance as a first class power has rested on millions of these same peasant soldiers.[3] Two of its greatest generals, Suvorov and Kutuzov, are still revered today for their accomplishments.

Failure to modernize the Russian armed forces during the late 1800's became obvious with Russia's humiliating defeat by the Japanese in 1905. Still, little action was taken to improve Russian capabilities, and the War of 1914 proved fatal for the Russian Imperial Army. The army began crumbling after serious defeats in 1915 and 1916. By the summer of 1917, the army had become an armed mob, and its angry, disillusioned, and very hungry soldiers were quite ready for peace—or revolt.

The collapse of the Imperial Army meant the collapse of the Russian Empire as provinces broke away in their attempt to become independent countries. Poland, Finland, and the Baltic republics made their escape from Russia. The Caucasus republics, Central Asian khanates, and Ukraine were not so lucky. Red Army units entered each country and they were swiftly Sovietized. Lenin clearly saw that a Russian state of any kind required a massive army, not merely to oppose foreign invaders, but to maintain tight control at home. Today's Russian Army, with its armored vehicles and ballistic missiles on transporter-erectors, may be thought of as Lenin's Red Army with high technology.

BY PERSUASION OR BY FORCE

The Red Army is said to have had two fathers. Most often, Leon Trotsky's[4] name is associated with the Red Army as it struggled

---

[3] An agrarian land, Russia failed to develop much industry or commerce until the Soviet era. Apart from military might, Russia's only other lever of power in global affairs lies in its ability to export oil and natural gas. Unlike China, which has a robust manufacturing and exporting economy, Russia is an exporter of raw materials.

[4] Trotsky was born Lev Davidovich Bronstein in 1879, headed the Red Army during the Civil War, was isolated politically by Josef Stalin in the 1920s, expelled from the CPSU in 1928, and finally murdered in Mexico City on Stalin's orders in August 1940.

against the White armies during the Russian Civil War. Although less well known, M.V. Frunze also can lay claim to the origin and shaping of the Red Army. Indeed, it was Frunze who battled Admiral Kolchak and later Baron Wrangel to help ensure the survival of the Soviet state.

Frunze was a contemporary of Felix Dzerzhinsky, first director of the Cheka, and shares credit with "Iron Felix" for the preservation of Bolshevism in Russia from its many enemies. *"Frunze conceived the 'unitary military doctrine,' combining ideology, determination, and aggressiveness in the promotion of world revolution."*[5]

After the Civil War, it was Frunze who initiated structural reforms, including the professional training of officers and the introduction of technical schools. Frunze also adapted remnants of the Russian Imperial General Staff Department for Secret Affairs into the Red Army's military intelligence branch. That would become known as the GRU in 1942.[6] Although Frunze died in late 1925, many of his innovations survived him and helped shape the Soviet Army of World War II and today's Russian army.

The Soviet state, which consolidated its rule over Russia, was a product of revolutionary armed force and secret police terror. Trotsky, Frunze, and Dzerzhinsky were revolutionary conspirators and agitators in Tsarist Russia. Somewhat in the mold of revolutionary France's Lazare Carnot, Trotsky and Frunze fused remnants of the Imperial Russian Army with revolutionary rabble, and turned the force into a formidable army that fought on as many as sixteen different fronts. It totaled three million men by the war's end in 1921. The Red Army's victory in a bloody civil war, combined with the Red Terror of the Cheka, might be considered the cradle of modern Russia. It is a heritage shared in part by today's Russian President Vladimir Putin, a former KGB officer.

---

[5] Wikipedia note.

[6] Fifth Department of the Russian Imperial General Staff for Secret Affairs. The Red Army absorbed a large number of former Tsarist officers and non-commissioned officers. "The Bolsheviks drew many of their best field commanders from the ranks of talented tsarist noncommissioned and junior grade officers whose plebian origins had slowed their promotions in an army that placed a premium upon birth and wealth." W. Bruce Lincoln, Red Victory: A History of the Russian Civil War, p. 84

In his 1917 work, *State and Revolution*, Lenin bluntly stated: "*A standing army and police are the chief instruments of state power.*"[7] Lenin and his Bolshevik associates viewed Soviet Russia as having enemies inside the country who must be liquidated. They also saw Russia as surrounded by imperialist powers which must be defeated or subverted. Put simply, the world consisted of two camps: the Bolsheviks who were certain they had history on their side, and all others. Others were not merely capitalists, but classical liberals, social democrats, and revolutionaries of other stripes who were considered class enemies and apostates.[8] To paraphrase Lenin and Trotsky, persuasion is never so effective as when it is backed by force and fear.

Before and during the Russian Revolution, the Bolsheviks firmly believed that it was their right and duty to spread Marxist-Leninist revolution to all points of the globe. Not only did they want to revolutionize the advanced capitalist countries, but also the toilers of the East. Lenin proclaimed himself not merely a Russian, but an internationalist. For this reason, he and Trotsky (then considered the Number Two man in the Bolshevik hierarchy) advocated a policy of world revolution.

For a brief period following the close of World War I, Marxist revolutions did break out in Hungary and parts of Germany. Communist agitation occurred in China and several European colonies. Agitation even took place in the United States with Comintern support for the Industrial Workers of the World (or IWW) known informally as the Wobblies—a radical labor union.[9] The IWW later became part of the new Communist Party in the USA.

Following Lenin's death and the political eclipse of Leon Trotsky, the CPSU de-emphasized world revolution, but Bolshevik support of Marxist groups outside Russia never stopped. The concept of a capitalist encirclement remained a staple of Soviet policy. Even

---

[7] Lenin, State and Revolution, (1917)

[8] The "Two Camp" doctrine is most often associated with Party theorist A.A. Zhdanov.

[9] The IWW, incorrectly known as the "International Workers of the World," was incorporated into the CPUSA.

today, some Russian diplomats will remind Americans of their armed intervention in Russia during 1918-1920. The memory may have faded, but the wound remains. Americans are completely ignorant of that intervention.

SWORD AND SHIELD

The Russian contribution to activities directed against the United States arises from a quite different set of historical factors than do those of China. Russian subversion has its roots in the revolutionary struggle of the late 19th century against the Tsarist government. Lenin recognized the impossibility of operating openly in an autocratic police state.

In his 1902 work, *What is to be done?*, Lenin advocated two adaptations to classical Marxist revolutionary theory.[10] The first was to employ conspiratorial methods to organize revolutionary cells among workers to avoid arrest and disruption by Tsarist police. The second was to recruit professional revolutionists thoroughly indoctrinated in Marxism who would organize cells and lead revolutionary workers. These individuals would become the vanguard.

The pattern of clandestine organization established in the early 20th century became the model for the international work of the Comintern after the Revolution of 1917. The Cheka, the ancestral body of today's SVR and FSB,[11] ferreted out political opponents at home and worked abroad in the 1920s to form or encourage Communist cells in China, various European countries, and even in North America.

As the sword and shield of the Revolution, the Cheka and its successors were called upon to defeat sabotage and subversion inside the Soviet Union, while spreading Communist influence abroad.

---

[10] "What is to be done?" V.I. Lenin, 1902; reprinted 1943, International Publishers, New York

[11] The Cheka, which takes its name from the Russian initials for Chrezvicheniya Kommisiya (the "Extraordinary Commission") gave rise in succession to the OGPU, NKVD, KGB, and today's SVR and FSB – Sluzhba Vnutrennikh Razvedki (Foreign Intelligence Service) and Federativnoye Sluzhba Bezopasnosti (Federal Security Service.) The Comintern (Communist International) was staffed by hardened Communists specially trained to recruit and organize foreigners to serve Communist interests. The GRU (Glavnoye Razvedivetelnoya Upravleniya) or Main Intelligence Directorate of the Russian army operates in cooperation with the SVR and FSB.

The Cheka adopted one tried and true operational method from its Tsarist predecessor, the Okhrana—the use of *agents provocateurs*. Under the Cheka's operational direction, *agents provocateurs* abroad assumed the external form of monarchists, liberal democrats, and others believed to be opponents of the Communist regime. Upon gaining the trust and confidence of the individual or group, the *agent provocateur* was then tasked to arrange for capture or murder of their target. They accomplished the task by luring individuals back to Russia—purportedly to meet with counter-revolutionary cells which did not exist—or by kidnapping the person, or simply using poison or a pistol to eliminate them. Since the Cheka's day, political murder has become more sophisticated, but is still in the SVR's playbook.[12] The object remains the same: to protect Russian leadership against challengers and to eliminate defectors with sensitive inside information on the leadership's inner workings.

The Russian state and society into which the Red Army and Cheka were born in 1918 was shaped by a thousand years of autocracy. Russia's 19th century historian, Nikolai Karamzin, described Russia as a "Byzantine-Christianized-Mongol" state steeped in centuries of despotism.[13] Indeed, the Mongol Golden Horde's rule of Russia left an indelible mark not only on the Russian gene pool, but on its psychology. An argument can be made that historically and ethnically Russia is more of an Asian than a European state. In all of Russian history, there was never any period even vaguely resembling the Renaissance or Enlightenment as there was in Western Europe, nor close to a Magna Carta or liberal democracy as in England. Force was always supreme.

Completely unlike China, Russia never developed a tradition of manufacturing and trading with long-distance commercial interests. Its rich lands were, however, ideally suited for large scale agriculture. The Russian Empire, primarily Ukraine, grew wheat and other grains

---

[12] Assassination remains a tool of the Russian leadership for eliminating political opposition. Examples include Lev Rebet and Stepan Bandera, Ukrainian nationalists (1950s); Georgiy Markov, Alexander Litvinenko, Sergei and Yuliya Skripal, to name but a few, and most recently the attempted poisoning of dissident Alexei Navalny.

[13] Karamzin himself (1766-1826) claimed Mongol ancestry with his name being a Russified version of "Kara-mirza." A witticism has it that "if you scratch a Russian you'll find a Tartar."

and was known as the breadbasket of Western Europe until 1913. Unfortunately, the oppressive Tsarist system was based on serfdom, and the vast majority of peasants were bound to a landlord and tied to the land.[14] The relatively few urban workers in Tsarist Russian cities were little better off than their rural cousins.

The terrible stresses of World War I, the breakdown of the economy and civil society, and the collapse of central authority under the pressure of war rendered society chaotic and ripe for revolt. Lenin, Trotsky, and Dzerzhinsky welcomed worsening conditions as they created an ideal atmosphere for seizure of power. The result was what amounted to a coup in wartime Petrograd in November 1917.

Given their conspiratorial backgrounds, it is safe to say that, from their perspective, "the worse the conditions, the better" in adversary countries like the United States. The Bolsheviki have faded into the past, but the Russian tradition of suspicion and hostility toward outsiders lingers on. To this day, the inner leadership circle considers the United States "*Glavniy Vrag,*"[15] or "the main enemy."

The Cheka is the defense of the revolution as the Red Army is;
as in the civil war the Red Army cannot stop to ask whether it may
harm particular individuals, but must take into account only one thing,
the victory of the revolution over the bourgeoisie, so the Cheka must
defend the revolution and conquer the enemy even if its sword falls
occasionally on the heads of the innocent.[16]

Felix Dzerzhinsky

---

[14] Only abolished in 1861 by the "Liberator Tsar" Alexander II, who was assassinated by terrorists in 1881.

[15] The United States unofficially became the "main enemy" in July 1943 after Nazi Germany's catastrophic defeats in Russia. At that time the Central Committee and General Staff concluded that the defeat of Germany was only a matter of time, but that the Soviet Union would face a new, more powerful enemy.

[16] Felix Dzerzhinsky, founder of the Cheka, predecessor of the KGB and today's SVR and FSB

PART TWO

PLUNDERING THE "MAIN ENEMY"

CHAPTER 4

CHINA'S NEW EMPIRE . . . OF SORTS

The Chinese government does not engage in theft of commercial secrets in any form, nor does it encourage or support Chinese companies to engage in such practices in any way.[1]

Xi Jinping

"The road to Paris runs through Beijing" is a phrase attributed to Lenin as he surveyed the potential for extending Bolshevik revolutionary power through the toilers of the East—the people of Asia and Africa—to overthrow their European masters. Figuratively, Lenin suggested that the way to defeat European capitalism was to encourage rebellion in Third World lands, and for the world Communist movement to make common cause with any new anti-colonial governments.

Beijing's present view of its Asian and African neighbors is far less revolutionary than in Mao's day, but similar in the sense that gaining influence in the Third World steadily reduces the power of Paris, London, and Washington. In keeping with Lenin's quip, China is moving systematically to encircle the West politically and, to some extent, militarily, by building ties with countries in the Third World.[2] Since Xi Jinping's 2013 speech in Kazakhstan, Beijing has launched the Belt and Road Initiative (BRI) which is aimed at

---

[1] Response to *"Does China's government hack US companies to steal secrets?"* by Mark Ward, www.bbc.com. September 23, 2015

[2] Author believes the best way to understand Chinese global strategy is by analogy with the ancient game of *wei-ch'i*. Unlike chess, which is directly confrontational with the capture of pawns and pieces leading to a checkmate, confrontation in *wei-ch'i* is indirect. Skilled *wei-ch'i* players only infrequently capture an opponent's tiles. Rather, a skilled *wei-ch'i* player will place his tiles in such a way as to increase his control of the board while methodically limiting that of his opponent. The defeated party resigns when it becomes clear that he is "boxed in" and unable to make any further meaningful move.

developing relationships with Third World (and some European) nations.[3] Xi declared the BRI to be a partnership in development, emphasizing infrastructure development that would lead to improved trade relationships. The BRI devotes major attention to building roads, railroads, oil and gas pipelines, public buildings, and especially seaports and harbors.

The key point to bear in mind is that the BRI is neither a trading bloc nor a free trade zone, but an extension of China's state power. Its goal is to gain political influence and geostrategic advantage. China's BRI relationships can be translated into political power in international bodies such as the United Nations, World Health Organization, Organization of African Unity, and many others. They also give Beijing a presence in areas it deems of strategic importance. An estimated quarter of a million Chinese serve overseas on various BRI projects. Detachments of China's naval and marine forces are discreetly posted in several locations.

Expanded ties through BRI have given China long term leases in key ports such as Piraeus in Greece, Haifa in Israel, Djibouti on the Horn of Africa, Gwadar in Pakistan, Darwin in Australia, Colon in Panama, and virtual ownership of Hambantota in Sri Lanka. Ties with Iran are especially important as that country is China's principal source of oil. Persian Gulf oil flows through the Strait of Malacca and the South China Sea to Chinese ports. Future moves may bring Mombasa in Kenya and Suva in Fiji into Beijing's collection of rented seaports.

China's first BRI move, unsurprisingly, was into Central Asia. Kazakhstan is a rich source of crude oil and Turkmenistan practically floats on natural gas. Moreover, the Central Asian states link China with Russia and South Asian states. Le Yueh-cheng, Vice Minister of Foreign Affairs, stated that *"the way to get rich"* is to build roads. China is helping Central Asians do just that.

China's next BRI move was to Africa where nearly all that continent's countries now are part of the Initiative. Most important of

---

[3] See Peter Frankopan's The New Silk Roads. There is an abundance of information on BRI in Foreign Affairs, publications of the Council of Foreign Relations, the German Marshall Fund, and many other sources.

the African nations for resources are Nigeria (China's second source of oil), Angola (its third source), and the Democratic Republic of Congo and Zambia which are sources of rare earths and metals like copper and cobalt, which are essential for making computers and electronics. Adding to their domestic production of rare earths, China now controls more than 80% of the world supply. China's Huawei Corporation has installed its Safe City surveillance technology in at least six African capitals.

Beijing's most recent area of activity has been in the South Pacific, Melanesia, and Papua New Guinea. Although some BRI-related effort has gone into the construction of public buildings or seaports, this move is of greater strategic importance than it is of economic importance. Fiji and Papua New Guinea are the countries of main interest to China.[4] Papua New Guinea lies immediately north of Australia, separating Australia from its U.S. allies and bases in the western Pacific, while Fiji sits squarely astride the vital sea lines of communication connecting America and Australia.

Moreover, China has enrolled BRI partners in the Middle East, the Balkans, and the Andean republics of South America. Most Americans are completely unaware that China has established a powerful presence at Colon, the Panamanian port at the Caribbean entrance to the Panama Canal. The Chinese recently established diplomatic ties with Nicaragua and have a presence in the Gulf of Fonseca. Beijing is increasingly active in Central America and the Caribbean, which is of great strategic importance to the United States. Trade aspects are necessary to China's economy and lucrative to its state-controlled firms, but even more significant is Beijing's ability to slowly but steadily box in the West.

Along with leases for ports in strategic locations, the Chinese have emphasized development of a 21st century high seas naval fleet. The People's Liberation Army Navy (PLAN) is fully capable of blue water operations in the Indian Ocean or Pacific Ocean. Their fleet includes submarines and at least two aircraft carriers. With

---

[4] Beijing recently dispatched police trainers to assist PM Sogavare of the Solomons to deal with riots allegedly caused by "Taiwanese agents." Chinese police trainers provide an entry point for further Chinese initiatives.

appropriate basing rights in ports distant from China, the PLAN is increasingly capable of globally projecting China's power. The PLAN was recently augmented by a PLA Marine Corps (PLAMC) fully capable of amphibious operations. PLAMC exercises with its Russian counterpart, known as the Black Death naval infantry.[5]

Without any fanfare, China has developed a new kind of empire which gives it global reach and the possibility of negatively affecting America's military and economic interests as close as the Panama Canal, or as distant as the Persian Gulf. This overseas empire and naval basing supports the observation by Colonels Qiao and Wang that if actual fighting were to break out, China would be well-positioned to counter any military moves by the U.S. or its allies *before the first shot is fired*. Remember, the Chinese end-game is the slow, methodical limitation of American influence overseas to such a degree that armed conflict would be inconceivable before it could begin. This is the application of Sun Tzu's ancient wisdom on a global scale.

THE CENTER OF THE WORLD—PAST AND FUTURE

Why is China conducting a multifaceted intensive campaign against the United States while slowly building a quasi-empire abroad in the Third World and in the oceans? Why aren't other countries doing the same, say India, Brazil, Japan, South Africa, or Germany? Why is it China?

It is important for westerners, Americans in particular, to gain an understanding of the wellsprings of China's current drive for expansion and its barely-concealed passive-aggressive attitude toward the United States. Their mindset goes far beyond Xi Jinping thought, or Mao thought, or even the imperatives of Leninism. Rather it is embedded in the history of China which stretches over four thousand years. More particularly, it stems from China's harsh experiences at the hands of the West after 1820.

In the middle of Tiananmen Square stands an imposing monument more than 100 feet tall. This monument is known formally

---

[5] David Lague, "Special Report: China expands amphibious forces in challenge to U.S. beyond Asia," Reuters, 20 July 2020.

as the Monument to the People's Heroes. Informally, it is known as the Monument to the Century of Humiliation.

This monument reminds all Chinese every day of the Century of Humiliation. The monument's unstated message is: "This will never happen again." Not only that, but the carved marble panels at the base of the monument remind all Chinese that it was imperialists from the outside, and traitors from within that brought China low. Put another way, it's not just a monument to honor past suffering, but a commitment to a better future.

This perspective is important to understand because it reveals much about the Chinese mindset, which was molded not merely by Communist ideology, but by two thousand years of history. In particular, the years roughly between 1839 and 1949, which was a highly unpleasant time for China, influences their thought. That very unpleasant century was a time of chaos, death, and exploitation of China by nearly all the western powers, as well as by Japan and Russia. America has a checkered part in the unpleasantness. Of course, Party propagandists have forgotten the positive points and emphasized the negative.

For millennia China had thought of itself as "Chung-kuo," the Central Kingdom. China considered itself the summit of civilization—T'ien-hsia, "All Under Heaven." In their thinking, there was nothing beyond China except for lesser kingdoms, semi-civilized tribes, and barbarians. China was vaguely aware of civilizations in India, Persia, and the Roman Empire, but mountains and deserts kept those lands distant and little known to the Chinese. For over 2,000 years, China had experienced a series of great empires which dominated much of East Asia—the Han, T'ang, Sung, Yuan, Ming, and Ch'ing (Qing.) The Central Kingdom had almost 3,000 years of rich literature and had made discoveries and great inventions in science, medicine, the graphic arts, astronomy, and philosophy.

Historically, China had two great fears. The first always was of fragmentation. The Chinese feared internal anarchy and division, and the lack of a strong central government. The collapse of great dynasties was often accompanied by civil war and division into warring units. The second great fear was of invading barbarians who threatened China's sense of order and stability. The Great Wall itself stands as a massive witness to repeated invasions from the north.

The latest wave of barbarian invaders, initially British, came from the sea. These invaders were perhaps the most formidable of all because they brought with them the seeds of fundamental social, political, economic, and cultural change that still are at work shaping China. Previous invaders, such as the Manchus and Mongols, were absorbed into Chinese culture. The new invaders, however, imposed their own cultural values on China, including their political forms and religions. *Marxism-Leninism is a European import no less than capitalism.*

The two-thousand year-old civilization began to break down under Western pressure. Little of the Confucian system survived into the 20th century. China reached its most abysmal depth in the 1920s as rival warlords crisscrossed the land, burning and looting, often with European or Japanese backing. That was followed by fourteen years of Japanese invasion.[6] In less than a century, China was reduced from greatness to abject poverty and foreign occupation. In many cases, its government, economy, and social patterns were utterly and forever destroyed.

From the late 19th century onward, the dream of Chinese nationalists, what would later become the Chinese Nationalist and Chinese Communist parties, was to restore China's territorial integrity and ancient status. Their common goal was to expel foreigners, end exploitation, build a new society along modern lines, create wealth, and ultimately resume China's position as the world's leading state. Both the Nationalists and Communists could agree on the goals to be achieved. Where they differed was on which road to take to achieve those goals.

The decision which road to take was reached on the battlefield between 1946 and 1949. The way chosen was that of Lenin, rather than of Sun Yatsen. China's fundamental decision was to turn to the Soviet Union rather than the West for help in modernizing China. Only after Mao's death and Deng Xiaoping's rise to power in 1978 could Beijing turn to the West for the capital, technology,

---

[6] This is reckoned from the 1931 invasion of Manchuria until Japan's surrender in 1945.

and markets to make China a Great Power. *Turning to the West, the United States in particular, did not mean that China's leaders had any intention of absorbing Western Enlightenment ideals along with their nanotechnology.*

What lurks beneath the surface is more than a century of anger and resentment that resulted from the western humiliation of China. The bitterness built up from a century of invasion, civil war, exploitation, chaos, and degradation remains a key element in the worldview of the People's Republic. It cannot be forgotten or ignored.

China's drive to equal and surpass the West receives at least some of its fuel from the legacy of the past. Today, the United States exemplifies the west, as Great Britain did in the 19th century. Xi Jinping intends for China to assume its rightful position as the world's leading power by 2030. He considers leading the world China's destiny, as well as his personal duty.

Many American and European Western leaders blithely assume that by sharing Western capital and technology to help China start its own economic engine, that China would somehow gradually liberalize its political structure and become a democratic country. The events of the Spring 1989 Tienanmen Pro-Democracy demonstrations, and the subsequent violent massacre should have signaled that liberalization was not a Communist Party goal. Instead of a liberal Chinese style democracy, perhaps like Taiwan, the People's Republic of China has now grown into a totalitarian giant whose object is the destruction of imperialist powers. The CCP's aim is to destroy the powers that made its growth possible. Their goal is imposition of China's global dominance—economically, technologically, militarily, and politically.

What emerges from Chinese doctrine, ancient or modern, is that China's preference is for a slow but steady strangling of its chief adversary. The Chinese ideally want to reach a point where American collapse or surrender is achieved with minimal bloodshed and physical damage. The chief weapons in their strategy are intelligence collection, especially focusing on theft of technology, and political-psychological subversion. The object in view is to erode American confidence in their own democratic heritage. They encourage Americans to disparage the instruments of Constitutional government, and reject their elected leaders. In a "battlefield beyond the battlefield," China intends for chaos in the American rear to lead to collapse at the front. This is strategy taken directly from *Sun Tzu Bing-fa*.

Generally in war the best policy is to take a state intact;
to ruin it is inferior to this.

Sun Tzu

CHAPTER 5

RUSSIA'S NEW KIND OF WAR

The United States is not only the strongest,
but also the most terrified country.

Leon Trotsky

The American people, who set the world an example in waging a
revolutionary war against feudal slavery, now find themselves in the
latest, capitalist stage of wage slavery to a handful of multimillionaires,
and find themselves playing the role of hired thugs who, for the benefit of
wealthy scoundrels, are throttling the Russian Socialist Republic on the
pretext of 'protecting' it from the Germans. We know that help from you
will probably not come soon, Comrade American workers, for the revolution
is developing in different countries in different forms and at different
tempos (and it cannot be otherwise).[1]

V.I. Lenin

German tanks were still burning on the fields at Kursk in July 1943 when Premier Josef Stalin and his inner circle made a secret decision of the highest importance. The Battle of Kursk was the greatest tank battle ever fought, resulting in a catastrophic Nazi defeat. From that point until the capture of the Reichstag in May 1945, the Soviet High Command reckoned that Nazi Germany would be defeated.

Almost without a second thought, Soviet Russia shifted its focus. Russia identified its new "main enemy"—*Glavniy Vrag*—which was none other than its ally, the United States of America.

From June 1941 to May 1945, the U.S. provided thousands of tons of supplies, including vehicles, critical materials, and food to its Russian "ally." The Russians eagerly accepted all of the aid and constantly badgered Washington for more assistance. Much

---

[1] From Lenin's April 1918 letter to the American workers

of the aid was shipped from Portland, Oregon, across the Pacific to Vladivostok in Soviet transports. At that time, Japan and the Soviet Union were observing the April 1941 nonaggression treaty which, ironically, Nazi Germany had brokered. Other tonnage arrived in the Persian Gulf and was transported through western Iran to Russia's Caucasus republics. Considerably more aid was shipped via the dangerous Murmansk Route, running the gauntlet of Nazi U-boats. American loss of ships and sailors was high.[2]

Meanwhile, back in the USA, Soviet moles were busily ferreting out American nuclear secrets. Only well after the war was the Rosenberg–Greenglass spy ring exposed, resulting in trials and executions. One Soviet spy, born in Iowa but brought up as a citizen in the Soviet Union, reentered the United States, enlisted in the U.S. Army, and wangled a position at Oak Ridge. There "Zhorsh" passed along classified knowledge of the Polonium triggers needed in nuclear bombs to his Russian case officer. The result of this treachery was the 1949 explosion of a Soviet atomic bomb.

Added to that was the case of Harry Dexter White, Assistant Secretary of the Treasury—and a Soviet spy—who revealed sensitive American policies of the Roosevelt and Truman Administrations. It is believed that White cost the American taxpayer $1 billion by providing the Soviets with the plates to print Marks for use in occupied Germany. The Soviets printed tens of millions of Marks, all redeemable by the U.S. Treasury and ultimately the American taxpayer.

From the 1920s and 1930s, many American Communists, such as Whittaker Chambers, Elizabeth Bentley, Alger Hiss, Lauchlin Currie, Gregory Silvermaster, and numerous others served in senior

---

[2] American World War II aid to the Soviet Union was valued in 1942 dollars at $11.3 billion (today's equivalent of $180 billion) and included *inter alia* 400,000 trucks and jeeps, 14,000 aircraft, 13,000 tanks, and 8,000 tractors in addition to immense quantities of food, clothing, and medical supplies. See Albert L. Weeks, "Russia's Life-Saver: Lend-Lease Aid to the USSR in World War II;" 2004

government positions, while working with the GRU and KGB as recruited spies.[3]

The point made is that the Russians view an alliance in a very different way than the U.S does. The Russians were quite prepared to accept what the U.S. gave them, but they did not hesitate to steal what was not proffered. This all began during World War II, while the U.S. was busily, and naively, touting a jocular "Uncle Joe" Stalin as our valiant Russian ally.

Such deviant behavior is deeply rooted in Russian tradition but was given concrete form in doctrinal pieces published between the 1960s and 1980s. In his essay, *Two Languages of War*, Robert Bathurst makes the following point:

> Enemies are inherent in the language of Soviet politics and are one of the dynamics of Soviet society. Far from leading to the disintegration of social order and authority which Dostoyevsky predicted in *The Devils*, this paranoid function of inventing enemies has been made one of the not inconsiderable organizing principles of the Soviet state, certainly of the military. The 'spies are everywhere' campaigns are a periodic feature of the Soviet press, and induce the panic about war and enemies in which some [part] of Soviet life is led.[4]

Russian behavior varies from an outward display of civility to sullen rudeness, but at all times beneath the surface is a barely concealed visceral hatred of the non-Russian world. Bathurst notes that the tension induced by Russian propaganda constantly agitates

---

[3] These and other Soviet moles gave fuel to the demagogue, Sen. Joseph McCarthy, who ranted for several years about Communists in high places in the U.S. Government. As with most such fanatics, his story was partly true. But McCarthy's ranting had the effect of stifling, rather than advancing, serious counterespionage investigations. See also the Venona decrypted Soviet intelligence cables sent from the U.S. to Moscow in World War II (1996.) The Venona decrypts identify a number of Soviet agents, but some remain unidentified to this day.

[4] Robert Bathurst, "Two Languages of War," in Soviet Military Thinking, Derek Leebaert, ed.; p. 29

the people, preparing them for the onset of war unleashed by the "imperialists," and justifying to the people the "need" to intervene with Russian military force in some subject or neighboring country.

> This theme, born in the conspiratorial world of the Russian leaders, was proclaimed by Lenin in 1902, when he warned, "We are surrounded on all sides by enemies, and we have to advance almost constantly under their fire." It has become central to Soviet military thought and has been used as a weapon in the forced transformation of the Soviet state into a military-industrial complex, as Seweryn Bialer called it.[5]

A CYBER WAR

The confrontation between East and West now taking place over Ukraine signals the advent of a new Age of Warfare, far removed from the bloody, smoking fields of Kursk and Prokhorovka, or the bloody sandy beaches of Normandy and Okinawa. It is perhaps the kind of war spoken of by Colonels Qiao and Wang quoted in the opening pages of this book.

As the Chinese colonels noted: *"Warfare is now escaping from the boundaries of bloody massacre, and exhibiting a trend towards low casualties, or even none at all, and yet high intensity. This is information warfare, financial warfare, trade warfare, and other entirely new forms of war, new areas opened up in the domain of warfare."*[6]

The tense situation now existing between the NATO powers, including the United States and the Russian Federation, came about through Vladimir Putin's deployment of an estimated 100,000 Russian soldiers on three sides of Ukraine, today an independent republic in eastern Europe. If war does erupt between Russia and the NATO powers, it will be fought in different ways on different continents, and it will be fought globally.

---

[5] Ibid., p. 29

[6] Qiao and Wang, op.cit. *The Russian invasion of Ukraine began after this draft was formally reviewed and DOES NOT conform to the strategy outlined by Cols. Qiao and Wang.*

In an especially prescient piece of reporting, Ms. Maggie Miller describes a likely crossfire of Russian and American cyber weapons aimed at damaging or destroying critical infrastructure, paralyzing the civil economy, and degrading military operational capabilities. Added to this prospect would be attacks against the financial sector and damaging cyber raids aimed at crippling federal and local governments.[7] Ms. Miller reminds us that Russian hackers exploited flaws in the SolarWinds company's software to invade systems in the United States and other countries without detection.

Ukraine is the obvious first target of Russian malice. Ukraine has for at least five centuries tried—usually unsuccessfully—to achieve and maintain independence. Whether by the Poles or the Russians, Ukraine was subjugated and made part of another state. Putin believes that if he is to achieve his dream of rebuilding a good portion of the old Russian Empire, he must inevitably subjugate Kyiv (Kiev) to Moscow's rule.

From the perspective of any Russian ruler, be it Catherine the Great or Vladimir Lenin, Ukraine is simply too valuable to permit it to remain independent. Under Tsarist rule, it was the breadbasket of Europe prior to World War I. It has significant coal and iron resources, and an industrious population of about 43 million people. Should Ukraine's population and resources be absorbed into the Russian Federation as Putin desires, Russia then would have a population of nearly 200 million and an improved agricultural base. Moreover, Russia's control of Ukraine would again permit it to play overlord of eastern Europe as it did in the days of Nicholas I and Josef Stalin.

Miller reports a drumbeat of attacks on Ukrainian government websites, malware planted in Kyiv's governmental systems, and the pressure of Russian cyber capabilities against Ukrainian military forces. She points out that while the threat to Ukraine's independence is obvious, there are implications for NATO in Russia's combined conventional and unconventional capabilities.

---

[7] Maggie Miller, "Russian invasion of Ukraine could redefine cyber warfare," Politico; 28 January 2022

While these instances raised concerns, they were only a hint of Russian cyber capabilities. In a full-scale cyber assault, Russia could take down the power grid, turn the heat off in the middle of winter and shut down Ukraine's military command centers and cellular communications systems. A communications blackout could also provide opportunities for a massive disinformation campaign to undermine the Ukrainian government.

Such a nightmare for Ukraine could not only give Russian President Vladimir Putin an avenue to victory, but also provide a sneak peek into the future of warfare. That future also holds implications for Washington if Putin launches cyber attacks against the U.S. to retaliate against any sanctions President Joe Biden may impose.[8]

By any measure, Ukraine's situation is perilous. With no defensible natural boundaries, three sides blocked by Russian tanks and infantry, Fifth Columnists busily at work inside the country, and very tenuous ties to its Western backers, a cyber assault may be enough to bring down the regime and its armed forces without further effort. Miller notes that earlier hacker attacks in 2015 and 2016 hit Ukraine's power grid. In 2017, Russian tech-ops officers used the NotPetya virus to disrupt banks and government agencies.[9]

EYES ON AMERICA

So what are the implications for the United States of Russia's new ability to wage a war beyond the battlefield? Part of the answer is found in Ukraine's experiences in the last five years. Another part of the lesson may be found here in the United States, and further lessons may be taken from the experience of countries such as Estonia, Georgia, and possibly Kazakhstan.

---

[8] Miller, op.cit.

[9] Miller, op.cit.

In the U.S., the shutdown of the Colonial Pipeline is a case study of Russian cyber capabilities. There is also the case of JBS Foods, in which the Russian hacking group "REvil" paralyzed the firm in Australia and the United States until a ransom of $11 million was paid.[10] Ms. Miller notes that the Cybersecurity and Infrastructure Security Agency (CISA) warned that Russian hackers are working to take down U.S. critical infrastructures such as power and water.[11]

The Russians despise the weak and defenseless. Estonia suffered Russian wrath when that country decided to remove a Soviet statue dating from World War II. The Russians carried out devastating cyber attacks that shut down both government and civilian websites in Tallinn.

Georgia faced its own electronic onslaught prior to Russia's armed invasion of 2008. Professing to protect the tiny Ossetian minority from supposed Georgian repression, Russia quickly defeated the small Caucasus republic. Russia ensured that Georgia did not move closer to the U.S. and the West. They also quietly shut down the only non-Russian oil and gas pipeline from the Caspian Sea to the West. *"[T]he Russian invasion of Georgia was preceded by a swarm of digital attacks that overwhelmed Georgia government websites with traffic and temporarily disabled them, including the website of the country's president."*[12]

A Russian cyber assault against Ukraine would go far beyond the taking down of the Ukrainian military command and control system. A full-blown attack would destroy the country's telecommunications system, freeze the financial and banking system, shut down rail and air transportation systems, cut off heat and electric power, cripple manufacturing and agricultural production, and could even affect Kyiv's water supply. As Ms. Miller noted ominously, *"But these attacks are nothing compared to what a full-blown physical invasion coupled with cyber warfare would look like on a scale the world hasn't fully reckoned with."*[13]

---

[10] The Wall Street Journal, 9 June 2021

[11] Miller, op.cit.

[12] Miller, op.cit.

[13] Miller, op.cit.

With its Ukrainian victim totally paralyzed, Putin would give the word to his generals to finish the job. Russian armor and mechanized infantry divisions would occupy much of Ukraine. Fifth Columnists, aided by Russian Spetsnaz, would quickly capture all strategic points in Ukraine. Airborne troops could land behind Kyiv and isolate the city. In a matter of weeks, Putin could ride triumphantly through Kyiv and Ukraine's independence would again be snuffed out.

To consolidate their blitzkrieg victory, the Russians would blanket Ukraine with propaganda and disinformation campaigns intended to mislead and intimidate the Ukrainian people, hastening their acceptance of Russian subjugation. The conquered land would be sealed off from the West and other neighbors as completely as it was under Batu Khan and the Golden Horde.

President Putin has made no secret that if the U.S. crosses his "red line" he will retaliate in an "unexpected and asymmetric manner." While he has mentioned the deployment of Russian missiles located in Cuba and Venezuela, Putin's remarks also signal the use of weapons of the "battlefield beyond the battlefield." The shutdown of the Colonial Pipeline was a mere trifle or sideshow.

The lesson that Americans must take from the foregoing is that Russians cannot escape being Russians and acting out what centuries of historical experience have taught them. Russia is the kind of country that, as a wartime ally in desperate need, accepted billions of dollars worth of American aid. That aid, in fact, preserved Soviet Russia from Nazi conquest. Yet, without a whit of shame, Russia did not hesitate to steal from that same generous "ally." Adding insult to injury, in the midst of war Russia branded their U.S. "ally" as their main enemy.

Russia is a country without a conscience and probably also lacks a soul.

> *We need to keep in mind who we are dealing with. These guys are not Boy Scouts. They are absolutely ruthless. They will do things that will ruin people and cause great harm. This is a serious thing. It's not just about making the lights go on and off.*

LTG Ben Hodges[14]

---

[14] Former commanding general, U.S. Army Europe (USAREUR)

PART THREE

THE QUIET CHINESE INVASION

CHAPTER 6

CHINA'S COURTING
OF INTELLECTUALS

The policy of letting a hundred flowers blossom and a hundred schools of thought contend is designed to promote the flourishing of the arts and the progress of science; it is designed to enable a socialist culture to thrive in our land. Different forms and styles in art can develop freely, and different schools in science can develop freely . . . We think that it is harmful to the growth of art and science if administrative measures are used to impose one particular style of art or school of thought and ban another.

Mao Tsetung, speech inaugurating
the Hundred Flowers Movement, 1957

China values brainpower. To its credit, the People's Republic of China has lifted millions of Chinese out of illiteracy. This alone is a great achievement worthy of praise. Omitting the violently anti-intellectual campaign conducted during the Great Proletarian Cultural Revolution (1966-1970), China has invested a lot into higher education. The Chinese hire foreign teachers at all levels and have sent tens of thousands of students abroad, mainly to U.S. and European universities. Some of its graduates are now world-class researchers in a variety of disciplines, mainly in the physical and biological sciences.

China also values the brainpower of other countries and has created several mechanisms for tapping into others' knowledge. Two of the better-known schemes Beijing uses to harvest the fruits of foreign intellect are the Confucius Institutes and the Thousand Talents program. Both programs are international in scope, though the majority of their activity is in the United States.

Confucius was one of China's greatest philosophers. Confucius, known as Master Kung, lived in the 5th century BCE in what is today the Shantung province. Master Kung taught the principles of justice and honesty, what he called "right relationships," in society and government. He urged princes to conduct themselves with benevolence toward their subjects. His concept was that the "superior man," through his education and virtue, was upright in his conduct and obliged by his rank to care for the people at large.

Although he was a minor government official in his day, and often ignored by power-hungry princes, Confucius taught many students during his lifetime and developed a large following after his death. Confucianism experienced periodic setbacks. For example, in 212 BCE China's first emperor, Ch'in Shih Huang-ti, murdered 460 Confucians and burned Confucian books. Even so, Master Kung's philosophy of good government and right conduct has persisted from Han times as China's official state ideology for more than 2,000 years.[1]

Every educated boy was expected to learn the *Analects,* or basic Confucian principles, before going on to higher levels of education and the Imperial Examinations. Even Mao Tsetung and Chou Enlai were taught Confucian principles at an early age. The Imperial Examinations, established during the Han dynasty, were abolished by the Ch'ing (Qing) dynasty in 1906.

Confucianism fell out of favor in the Republic of China as scholars searched for other philosophies to guide the nation's governance. The Republic of China attempted to follow western liberal and constitutional forms, at least on paper. China's constitutions drafted after 1928 incorporated Dr. Sun Yatsen's work, *Three Principles of the People*, with western-style institutions and separation of powers.

Other modernizers, Chou and Mao among them, believed China's future lay in Marxism-Leninism. The formation of the Chinese Communist Party in 1921 presaged a Leninist centralization of power in a Party Central Committee and its Chairman. In 1935, at the Tsunyi (Zunyi) Conference, Mao became that Chairman, a position he retained until he died in 1976.

---

[1] The books were publicly burned and the scholars buried alive. Confucian principles were at sharp odds with the near-totalitarian Legalist governmental system of the Ch'in. The Ch'in collapsed a few years later to be replaced by the Han dynasty which re-instituted Confucian ethics and established the famous examination system.

Master Kung was out of favor in China for many decades. Confucianism's lowest point came during the Great Proletarian Cultural Revolution when the sage was reviled and held up as the antithesis of Revolutionary virtue. Red Guards even smashed his tombstone and, as in Ch'in dynasty times, burned his books. Confucianism went from being the official state ideology of China to being hailed as "stinking sewage."

Jian Junbo, writing for the former *Asia Times Online*, reminds us that the Chinese Communist Party under Chairman Mao criticized Confucian teachings as *"rubbish that should be thrown into the ash heap of history."* Since 2004, the Party has adapted a rehabilitated image, but not the substance, of Master Kung as *"an assistant to the Chinese god of wealth (and a representative of Chinese diplomacy), but not a tutor for [the] Chinese soul."*[2]

After more than a century of political oblivion, Confucius made his cautious return. In his new form, established in 2004, Confucius was made to serve the state interests of the People's Republic of China and the Chinese Communist Party. Some 400 Confucius Institutes have been established in 88 countries, though some have been closed due to overt pressures such as the Party's requirement to recognize the PRC as the sole, legitimate government of China. The PRC pressures the institutions to cut all contact with Taiwan, and to ignore American complaints regarding restrictions on students' academic freedom.

According to Professor David Shambaugh of George Washington University, Confucius Institutes were created as extensions of the Chinese Communist Party's Propaganda Department which funds the institutes abroad through Ministry of Education channels.[3]

Although the number of institutes in the United States has declined in recent years from its peak total of 117, the number affiliated with U.S. colleges and universities remains between thirty and fifty. The institutes enroll non-Chinese students in Mandarin language

---

[2] Jian Junbo, Asia Times Online, 9 October 2009

[3] David Shambaugh, "China's Propaganda System: Institutions, Processes, and Efficacy" China Journal (57), 2007, pp.49-50. Another source claims the Party's "United Front Work Department" directs the institutes.

and cultural programs. Many Confucius Institutes are located on college campuses, in contrast to German Goethe Institutes or French Alliance Francaise clubs, which are usually off-campus.

There have been persistent accusations of the Confucius Institutes being used as platforms for espionage and influence operations. Complaints and concerns have been raised that the Confucius Institutes are merely a pleasant-sounding cover for PRC intelligence activities, particularly covert influence campaigns, and the spotting and assessing of potential collaborators in foreign lands. Some authorities believe that the institutes also serve as watchdogs on Chinese university students and researchers. The presence of a senior Huawei official at the Confucius Institute at the University of Texas campus in Dallas was a cause for concern, though a security review did not uncover evidence of espionage.

Whether or not the Confucius Institutes in the United States or other countries conduct much in the way of industrial or political espionage, the fact remains that they serve as effective platforms for spreading Chinese propaganda directly to students at the university level, and they also identify persons who may be useful to the Chinese intelligence service.

Another means for Beijing to make productive use of foreign intellectuals is through their Thousand Talents program. The Thousand Talents scheme ostensibly connects selected foreign scientists, engineers, or biologists with a partner institution in China. Generous grants are proffered and lucrative opportunities are presented to foreign talents of interest to Beijing.

Recent press reports reveal Beijing's widespread effort to buy the support of intellectuals across the globe. Because intellectuals carry considerable weight as opinion makers and influencers, in addition to the expertise they can impart, the Chinese believe the Thousand Talents investment is a good use of their money.

Swiss police and Bern's Federal Intelligence Service have detected Chinese efforts to use LinkedIn and other social media to identify and contact Swiss intellectuals and professionals. Chinese tech-ops officers reportedly use fake profiles as bait to lure prospects. These profiles are used to establish ties with researchers, decision-makers, parliamentarians, civil servants, army personnel, bank employees, and academics." Once a target has taken the bait, the Chinese intelligence service seeks personal, privileged information of an economic, technical, or political nature. "*Those who comply are rewarded with monetary bribes as well as invitations and free entry to conferences in China.*"[4]

This practice also appears common in the United States. One particularly high profile case, documented by Reuters, the New York Times, and other sources, was that of former Harvard professor Charles M. Lieber. Lieber had been Chairman of Harvard's chemistry department. In Court, Professor Lieber admitted to taking "tens of thousands of dollars" from China. What is significant is that Dr. Lieber was renowned in the fields of nanotechnology and nanoscience. He was named the *"leading chemist in the world for the decade 2000-2010 by Thomas Reuters"*[5] for the importance of his research. He had been recruited into the PRC's Thousand Talents program. Today he is a convicted felon.

During his FBI interrogation, Dr. Lieber stated that the Chinese university he collaborated with under the Thousand Talents program had lots of money. *"That's one of the things China uses to try to seduce people."*[6] Although Dr. Lieber's case was sensational given his prominence in the scientific community, it is quite likely that there are many other American, European, and Asian scientists just like him.

Although the implication of espionage and the certainty of the transfer of Harvard's nanotechnology research to China are important, it is even more significant to note the ability of the PRC intelligence services to reach and recruit intellectuals of stature and achievement. These individuals become agents of influence within

---

[4] German Marshall Fund; "Chinese intelligence services use LinkedIn to extract intelligence from Swiss citizens;" Alliance for Securing Democracy of the German Marshall Fund; https://securingdemocracy.gmfus.org

[5] Wikipedia, Charles M. Lieber, so recognized in 2011

[6] Ellen Barry, New York Times, "In a Boston Court, a Superstar of Science Falls to Earth," 21-22 December 2021. Lieber had been arrested 28 January 2020. Two of his associates, Hongjie Dai and Peidong Yang, were not charged but may also have been associated with the Thousand Talents program. Nanotechnology is the ability to control matter at the atomic level, specifically structures at or below one hundred nanometers. Nanotechnology is used in metals, polymers, ceramics, and biomaterials.

their discipline and spotters of potential sources for the Chinese case officers involved in the operation.

CHARMING AMERICA AT THE STATE LEVEL

In recent years, China began recognizing the value of state and local political leaders and has opened a charm offensive to woo governors, mayors, and members of state legislatures. China understands that many of these individuals are influential in their hometowns and localities; otherwise, they would not be in office in a democratic system like that of the United States. Put another way, these leaders can serve as key communicators with members of their immediate political base, and perhaps to a degree with the broader community which they serve.

Being eminently practical, the Chinese believe that by positively influencing American officeholders, they can reach far broader audiences otherwise inaccessible to them. Hence, a charm offensive saves both resources and time while influencing American public opinion. In recent years, Beijing launched what might be called a leader engagement campaign in the United States at the subnational level. As with all such leader engagements, the object is to build rapport with local leaders while projecting a positive image. China hopes to parry good relations with governors, mayors, and other leaders into a quiet form of political power aimed upward at influencing America's national policy and downward at garnering support from the man on the street.

Chinese analysts of the American scene often realize there is a pronounced difference in the focus of subnational leaders than the view at the national level in Washington, D.C. Apart from the obvious differences in party affiliation, there are considerable differences in the types of issues leaders from each level face. Reflecting the famous quip of Tip O'Neill, "All politics is local," governors, mayors, and legislators are concerned with problems of employment, taxes, utilities, housing, streets, education, and similar local issues.

The distinct difference between the perspective of leaders in Washington is obvious to Beijing. National leaders are concerned with issues of national security. Those at the state and local level are more concerned with jobs and income. Beijing may find itself in an advantageous position to drive a wedge between the different levels of government if it can offer attractive economic deals to a region, state, or city.

A case in point is China's offer to buy grain in Iowa—a powerful inducement that could well influence state leaders to urge Washington to modify policies relating to Beijing. Speaking in Seattle to a group of U.S. governors in 2015, Xi Jinping stated: *"Iowa is known as the granary of the U.S. and Oregon is also a major producer. These two states can strengthen their cooperation with big agricultural producers like Shaanxi, Hebei, and Heilongjiang provinces."* He went on to extol Hewlett-Packard's set-up of a computer production center in Chongjing and dangled the prospect that Michigan's automotive industry might find profitable deals in China.[7]

> Xi emphasized that increased economic ties to China would deliver what American voters want most: jobs. "I know as governors, you are most concerned about employment. Cooperation [with China] in the above-mentioned areas will promote growth and create jobs, thus bringing benefits to our peoples."[8]

For governors with high unemployment rolls who face tough re-election campaigns, these visions of lucrative deals with Beijing involving contracts, purchases, and jobs are powerful siren calls. A few days following the governors' meeting, Xi met with then-Iowa Governor Terry Branstad.[9] A short time later, a Chinese trade delegation appeared in Des Moines to sign contracts for soybeans and other agricultural products. Fulsome in his praise, Governor

---

[7] Emily de La Bruyère and Nathan Picarsic, "All Over the Map: The Chinese Communist Party's Subnational Interests in the United States," Foundation for the Defense of Democracy, 15 Nov 2021; www.fdd.org/analysis/2021/11/15/all-over-the-map/

[8] ibid.

[9] In 2017 then-President Trump named Branstad as Ambassador to China. Branstad claims a relationship with Xi Jinping going back to 1982.

Branstad stated, *"This builds upon a long line of experience we have had together."*[10] In the same interview, Branstad carefully side-stepped broader national and international issues:

Referencing the growing U.S.-China tensions over the South China Sea, cyber security, trade issues, and human rights, Branstad further noted that he respected *"the fact that those issues have to be resolved at a national level. My role as a governor is to build those relationships, increase trade, and create more jobs in Iowa, those kinds of things."*[11]

The Iowa example amply demonstrates the subtle pressure Beijing can bring on the United States Government through its clever manipulation of state and local leaders and issues, mainly economic issues. Governor Branstad was in an uncomfortable position in which he was forced to distance himself from national policy to satisfy local needs. Beijing has taken Tip O'Neill to heart and used soybeans and wheat to offset inconvenient truths regarding cyber operations, human rights abuses, and the manipulation of American public opinion.

CHARMING TOURISTS

China is one of the most fascinating countries on Earth. With a history stretching over at least four thousand years, nearly every city and province has its historical monuments, ancient buildings, or important locations. The lush landscape and karst topography of southern and southwestern China is some of the most beautiful in the world. Moreover, everyone loves pandas. Finding something of interest to visit or film in China is hardly challenging. China is delighted to exhibit its treasures, and rightly so. China is a fascinating country with much to see.

Unsuspecting tourists don't realize they are also targets of Beijing's charm offensive. Visitors to China are treated to carefully scripted tours. Luxingshe, China's counterpart to Russia's Intourist, works

---

[10] La Bruyere, op.cit.

[11] La Bruyere, op.cit.

closely with the Public Security Bureau and orchestrates nearly all foreign visits.

Thousands more people will view China through a camera lens. What the audience will never see, and may never even suspect, is the very careful selection of the scenes and people featured, and the equally careful choreographing of what is said and done. After all, the Chinese People's Republic is a totalitarian state where nothing is left to chance. Everything is scripted and carefully reviewed. Filming of scenery, people, or ancient sites is done less to inform than it is to influence.

As with American advertising, the infomercial is not intended merely to educate or amuse, but to induce a viewer to buy. So it is with Chinese tourist films or Luxingshe tours. The product is China's beneficent role in a cheerful world. Tourism and film are merely part of the broad effort to checkmate or blunt the American policies or criticisms China deems harmful to its interests.

Hold your friends close, but hold your enemies closer.
Don Corleone, The Godfather

CHAPTER 7

HANGING THE CAPITALISTS

The capitalists will sell us the rope we will use to hang them.

V.I. Lenin, attributed

The contradiction between imperialism and the Chinese nation, and the contradictions between feudalism and the great masses of the people, are the principal contradictions in modern Chinese society. The great revolutions of modern and contemporary China have emerged and developed on the basis of these fundamental contradictions.

Mao Tsetung

It is said Lenin once quipped that capitalists would sell the rope that Communists would use to hang them. Neither Lenin nor Mao had the money or wit to arrange for such rope purchases; however, as events proved, Deng Xiaoping had exactly the right formula for acquiring the capitalists' rope, and the capitalists paid for it.

American corporate collaboration with the Chinese defense industry *was and is quite real.* Although some collaboration may have been unwitting, perhaps even unknown to senior executives of companies involved, *collaboration is undeniable.* Whether directly aiding the development of advanced weaponry, such as air-to-air missiles or avionics, or indirectly aiding by helping China sell garden tools in the United States to earn foreign exchange, American industry cannot avoid the charge of complicity. *Even if collaboration involved nothing more than providing technical data, training, or plant visits, U.S. corporations aided and abetted China's rapid progress toward its goal of military supremacy.*

The role of American banks is less clear in terms of weapons development but is still important to China's overall economic development. Backing from Goldman-Sachs and other major institutions facilitated the purchase or licensing of western technology and, in some cases, factories or entire corporations. A case in point is the Chinese acquisition of Motorola, today known as Lenovo.

In the last twenty years, technology transfer from the U.S. to China has continued at a steady pace. Apple Corporation transferred its state-of-the-art Fremont, California, plant to China. Hewlett-Packard and Seagate also have important facilities in China. Oxford Professor Peter Frankopan estimates the outflow from the United States to be a minimum of $225 billion USD per year, and likely significantly higher.[1]

What America's corporate executives fail to understand is the Chinese Communists' deep-set, but carefully hidden hostility toward foreigners in general, and toward Western political values and ideals in particular. The People's Republic of China has neither moderated its attitudes toward foreigners nor reigned in its aggressive external policy, which is deeply rooted in its ideology and history, as it strives to achieve its perceived national goals.

Pragmatically, the Chinese will absorb and use what they need from Corporate America. When there is little more to be drained or squeezed from the relationship, the foreign company will be forced out of business or simply taken over.[2] Outright seizure of Western assets would be certain in the event of open hostilities. At that point, it would simply be a matter of arresting any remaining American or foreign executives, probably on espionage charges, and placing the nationalized factories under direct Communist Party control.

Sun Tzu himself observed, *"Generally in war the best policy is to take a state intact; to ruin it is inferior to this."*[3] China does not wish to see a nuclear-burned wasteland in North America. Beijing fully appreciates the abundance of North America's natural resources. Its goal is not to destroy, but to absorb. Beijing would prefer to bring

---

[1] Peter Frankopan, The New Silk Roads, Alfred A. Knopf, New York, 2019. One wonders how much longer this theft can go on before there is nothing left worth stealing.

[2] Houston Chronicle columnist Chris Tomlinson gave an example of a French retailing company that entered China in 1995 with its required Chinese "partner." As the years passed, they found the partner prospered whereas the French firm barely held its own. Finally, after some twenty years in business in China, the French company was forced to sell 80% of its holdings to its partner.

[3] Sun Tzu as quoted in S.B. Griffith (trans) The Art of War, p. 77.

America's industry, or what remains of it, and natural resources under its full control. In Premier Li Keqiang's ideal view of the world of 2030, America would become an economic province tied to the Chinese technological and industrial heartland.[4] Corporate America, ignorant, greedy, and naive, is doing what it can to make China's national dream of world supremacy come true.

CORPORATE AMERICA SEEKS QUICK PROFIT

Like Lenin and Stalin before him, Mao failed to defeat America and Western capitalism. Mao's successor, Deng Xiaoping—reviled by the Red Guards as "the leading capitalist roader" during the Great Proletarian Cultural Revolution—chose a very different path for defeating the capitalist West. Deng's approach was very much in the tradition of Sun Tzu: do not destroy the enemy, but absorb him intact.

Under Deng's "Four Modernizations" effort, China turned to the United States for technology and capital. Corporate America, thinking to make huge profits selling to China's market of more than a billion customers, rushed right in to invest and harness cheap, Party-disciplined Chinese labor.

Most companies failed to find a pot of gold in the Chinese market, but the opportunity to make cheap products for the American market was still attractive. In the 1990s, American purchases of Chinese-manufactured goods soared, bringing untold wealth to China. Sometimes Chinese prosperity was at the cost of increasing American unemployment and forced closure of stateside factories.

China welcomed the incoming foreign firms. These were of critical importance to China's phenomenal economic expansion. Although companies from nearly every major industrialized country maintain facilities in China, pride of place goes to the American corporations. For example, the American Chamber of Commerce in China ("AmChamChina") lists no fewer than 1,200 firms, great

---

[4] Li Keqiang outlined his vision of America's future to then-President Donald Trump and an American delegation during a 2017 visit to Beijing. Premier Li was being completely candid and straightforward.

and small, doing business in China.[5] Added to that number are several hundred European and Japanese firms.

The U.S. roster reads like a page out of Forbes. America's most prominent corporations, many of which are engaged in American defense production or defense-related technology, now operate in China. They include Honeywell, Intel, Dell, Microsoft, Harris-Simpson, IBM, Boeing, GMC, Merck, Dow Chemical, Exxon-Mobil, Terex, General Electric, DuPont, Perkin-Elmer, Rockwell, Apple Computer, Cisco Systems, Hewlett-Packard, Juniper Networks, Oracle, Qualcomm, and dozens of other less well-known companies.[6] Each guest company is paired with one or more Party-owned enterprises and is, at least to some degree, sharing its technology and research with those entities.[7]

Underpinning the American collaboration are Wall Street financial leaders such as Goldman-Sachs, Bank of America, American Express, Citibank, Bloomberg, Ernst and Young, JPMorgan Chase, Lazard, Moody's Investor Service, S&P Global, Bank of New York Mellon, State Street Corporation, The Prudential Insurance, The Carlyle Group, PricewaterhouseCoopers, and many others.[8]

The banking and financial entities all have close ties with China's banking system, which is entirely under state control and the supervision of the Party Central Committee. While the extent of exposure of U.S. banks to Chinese institutions is unknown, what can be said is that bank-to-bank relationships enable China to pursue its Belt and Road Initiative and promote its defense modernization drive. American investments and bank exposures are in the hundreds of billions of dollars. All of this, it must be noted, is completely at risk. The Chinese Communist Party could take everything with a stroke of a pen.

---

[5] AmChamChina website.

[6] From AmChamChina's membership rolls.

[7] Most companies are required to have a partner or "sponsor" in order to have a presence in China. There have been documented occasions in which the Chinese sponsor ended up digesting its foreign partner. A recent press report indicates that Intel, Google, and Yahoo, among others have left China.

[8] AmChamChina, op.cit.

The rewritten constitution makes legal provision for foreign enterprises and investments in Article 18:

> Article 18. The People's Republic of China permits foreign enterprises, other foreign economic organizations and individual foreigners to invest in China and to enter into various forms of economic cooperation with Chinese enterprises and other economic organizations in accordance with the law of the People's Republic of China. All foreign enterprises and other foreign economic organizations in China, as well as joint ventures with Chinese and foreign investment located in China, shall abide by the law of the People's Republic of China. Their lawful rights and interests are protected by the law of the People's Republic of China.[9]

Nicely written, Article 18 provides legal protections (on paper) for American and western companies operating facilities in China; however, there are strings attached to these protections. As easily as Article 18 was written, it could just as easily be abrogated. Wall Street does not seem to recognize that threat yet.

The perspectives of western corporations and the ruling Chinese Communist Party are vastly different. Most westerners have profit in mind and are mesmerized by the prospect of 1.4 billion customers, a truly immense but ephemeral market. Western companies often believe they have to be in China because their competitors have a presence there. Many U.S. companies accept the sharing of their production technology and proprietary information with their Chinese hosts as a necessary cost of doing business. The loss is accepted in the hopes of greater access to China's market and the imagined profits foreign companies hope to make.

Some corporations invest in plants and machinery thinking of exploiting China's enormous, and strictly disciplined, labor pool. Such companies are delighted to pay Chinese laborers pennies on the dollar instead of what American workers would demand. The

---

[9] Constitution of the People's Republic of China, Art. 18

goal is volume production at the lowest possible cost, with profits coming from American sales. Some American companies are blind when it comes to the matter of exploiting goods produced by what amounts to slave labor. All are careful to mute any criticism of China.

By contrast, the Communist perspective is strengthening the power of the state. China's experience of foreigners on Chinese soil since the 1840s has not been positive, and foreigners are viewed with both distrust and distaste. China will accept foreigners only as long as they can be used either to generate hard currency earnings or to the extent that they share production technology and trade secrets. The Communist Party views the foreign presence as a necessary evil with a finite and limited existence. Contracts often stipulate that factories and expertise become exclusive Chinese property upon certain dates.

From which may be drawn a general rule, which never or very seldom fails, that whoever is the cause of another becoming powerful, is ruined himself.[10]

Niccolo Macchiavelli

---

[10] The Prince, Chapter 3

PART FOUR

RUSSIAN SPIES AND PROPAGANDA

CHAPTER 8

PROPAGANDA VIA SOCIAL MEDIA

*They identify an issue that they know that the American people feel
passionately about on both sides and then they take both sides and spin
them up so they pit us against each other. And then they combine that
with an effort to weaken our confidence in our elections and our
democratic institutions, which has been a pernicious and asymmetric
way of engaging in . . . information warfare.*[1]

FBI Director Christopher Wray

In a 1923 speech, Josef Stalin noted that print was the Communist
Party's "sharpest and strongest weapon." In pre-Revolutionary
Russia, the disaffected intelligentsia produced numerous subversive
pamphlets, leaflets, broadsheets, and journals to reach like-minded
individuals. After 1917, publications were a key part of the effort by
Lenin and his associates to build the subversive movement which
became the Communist Party of the Soviet Union (CPSU.)

Since the Revolution, the Party has used its sharpest weapon—
propaganda—to recruit millions of new followers, especially in the
Third World. As well, they aim to sow disinformation by undermining
Western governments. Print remains the SVR's main weapon, but
today it is disseminated electronically.

An ingrained belief held over from Bolshevik times is that there
can be no true state of peace between Russia and its adversaries.
In his 1962 work, *Military Strategy*, Vasily Sokolovskiy, Marshal of
the Soviet Union, stated: *"In a war period, the political struggle is
transferred from nonmilitary to military form."*[2] The Russians make no
distinction between war and peace as the concepts are understood

[1] Testimony, FBI Director Christopher Wray, 5 February 2020, reported by Eric Tucker in AP News, "FBI Director warns of ongoing Russian 'Information warfare'."

[2] Quoted in Soviet Perceptions of War and Peace, p.19 1981 NDU Press; Graham D. Vernon, ed.

in the West. Hostility is ever-present; only the means by which hostility manifests itself changes.

The Leninist view says the struggle against imperialism is continuous. Occasionally, the struggle plays out by means of armed force, but the fight is ongoing and relentless even in times of peace. Massive military power has its value and can be used to intimidate or coerce countries as diverse as Kazakhstan, Georgia, the Baltic republics, or Ukraine. *But how does one disrupt and destroy nations far from the nearest Russian tank?*

The nonmilitary form of struggle is known in Russian as *"aktivnoye meropriyatiye"* or *"active measures."* These nonmilitary actions involve a wide range of covert activities, from propaganda to assassination. For the Russians, if tanks are inappropriate to the situation, active measures make an admirable substitute, good for all seasons. *The condition of war never varies; only the means.*

SOCIAL MEDIA

With the explosion of social media in the 1990s, the Russians have adapted propaganda techniques to this new electronic platform. For First World audiences, classical print media—such as newspapers, magazines, or books—is no longer the propagandist's weapon of choice.[3] Rather, electronic media has displaced print due to its ability to instantly reach tens of millions of people, often with the shock power of images that old-fashioned print media could seldom match.

The Department of Homeland Security (DHS) noted in its May 2019 "Interim Report of the Countering Foreign Influence Subcommittee" that Russia had made social media a prime target of its various disinformation campaigns. Through an organization called the Internet Research Agency, the Russians exploited social media with tens of thousands of "news" stories, many of which were totally fabricated. Particularly damaging are messages DHS tactfully describes as "socially divisive content." These posts, approved by the highest levels of the Russian government, are intended to stir

---

[3] Print does remain important, and is especially important in Third World countries.

racial animosity and provoke clashes.[4] Social media propaganda is one aspect of Russian "active measures" and is clearly a campaign carried out as if planned by the Russian Army.

Although Moscow disavows any connection with this new sharp weapon, just as they denied connection with hackers responsible for the Colonial Pipeline shutdown, it is inconceivable to believe that the Internet Research Agency (IRA) operates in Russia entirely as it pleases and completely unknown to the FSB. DHS states the following: *"IRA has been identified as an entity with links to the Kremlin."*[5]

DHS also notes that Facebook reported Russian disinformation posted by the Internet Research Agency—an arm of the GRU—had directly reached 140 million of its American users.[6] Before social media, it was unimaginable that a propagandist, Communist or otherwise, would have the ability to reach such a huge audience.

Sometime in the late 1990s, Russian disinformation campaigns fundamentally changed their nature from obvious, sometimes heavy-handed denigration efforts, to a far more subtle tactic. Now, Russians use trolls and bots to quietly mislead Americans online. When deemed necessary, they don't hesitate to corrupt information in databases. Moreover, the absence of screening mechanisms or other safeguards on American social media platforms has allowed the Russians a virtual playground.

In its Interim Report, DHS states: *"Multiple IRA [ed. Russian]-controlled Facebook groups and Instagram accounts had hundreds of thousands of U.S. participants and that 170 Instagram accounts had posted approximately 120,000 pieces of content. In November 2017, a Facebook employee testified that Facebook had identified 470 IRA-controlled accounts that had collectively made over 80,000 posts over two and a half years to August 2017."*[7]

---

[4] DHS, op.cit., pp. 17-18

[5] Department of Homeland Security (DHS) "Interim Report of the Countering Foreign Influence Subcommittee," 27 May 2019, p. 18

[6] DHS, op.cit., p. 27

[7] DHS, op.cit, p. 22

For its part, Twitter also appears vulnerable to the spread of Russian disinformation. DHS notes that: *"Twitter is a smaller platform but due to its design [it] still carries a larger portion of the blame for disinformation sharing; its product is information and it is easy to understand how to use it for disinformation campaigns. Research is a simpler task than some other platforms and therefore this gives the impression that their data is more accessible."*[8]

The point Homeland Security makes is that social media platforms, in their effort to be popular with American users lend themselves beautifully to clever exploitation by Russian entities. The Russians do not care which side of a divisive political or social issue is the correct one, or which opinion prevails. That is irrelevant for them. What matters is the extent of the enmity and discord they can create.

THE AUTOMATION OF PERSUASION

With the widespread popularity of the Internet and social networking websites, at least two ubiquitous creatures have come to inhabit today's digital world—one human, one artificial. Each is new to the covert influence game, and Chinese and Russians use both to attack the West.

The human inhabitant of this digital world is called a troll. This is a person motivated either by ideology, monetary gain, or plain nastiness. Trolls can operate under their own or assumed identities and have no responsibility for the sourcing or veracity of the information they post. They post material on the Internet with the intention of manipulating viewers' perceptions, confusing or distorting issues, deliberately planting falsehoods, or in hope of sparking conflict through hostile or inflammatory messages.

China hires trolls, known as Fifty Centers, to post messages favorable to China or derogatory of the United States. The goal of the Fifty Centers—who reportedly are paid fifty cents for each post—is to promote a positive image of the Chinese Communist Party and the People's Republic of China. The operational objective

---

[8] ibid., p. 22

of the Chinese intelligence service, which sponsors this army of influencers, is to mold American public opinion to favor Beijing's views on bi-lateral or international issues.

The artificial inhabitant of the digital world is the bot, short for robot. A bot can be either helpful or highly damaging. Helpful bots are programmed to scan millions of documents to aid researchers in finding the necessary information. As a labor-saving device, this category of helpful bots aid researchers in more quickly locating the information they seek.

The highly damaging bot is a creature whose mission is to delete, degrade, or deceive through alteration of existing documentation. Hostile intelligence services and hackers program damaging bots to achieve specific operational ends, such as inserting false or doubtful information, collecting sensitive information belonging to an adversary, or erasing information considered inimical to their interests. The Chinese and Russians have a well-funded team of computer experts well versed in the use of bots.

> While most bots are used for productive purposes, some are considered malware, since they perform undesirable functions. For example, spambots capture email addresses from website contact forms, address books, and email programs, then add them to a spam mailing list. Site scrapers download entire websites, enabling unauthorized duplication of a website's contents. DoS bots send automated requests to websites, making them unresponsive. Botnets, which consist of many bots working together, may be used to gain unauthorized access to computer systems and infect computers with viruses.[9]

A publication titled "Bad Bot Report 2021: The Pandemic of the Internet" somewhat contradicts the above information by stating that, a *quarter* of all internet traffic (25.6%) in 2021 consisted of "bad" bots, whereas only 15.2% were considered "good." Human operators

---

[9] Wikipedia.

accounted for the balance of 59.2%—a decrease brought about by the proliferation of bots, both good and bad.[10]

The report noted that the most frequent targets of bad bot traffic were, in order: Telecom and ISPs, computing and IT, sports, news, and business services. Bad bots can take over accounts and scrape for proprietary data.

> Moderate and sophisticated bad bots still constitute the majority of bad bot traffic. Categorized as Advanced Persistent Bots or APBs, these accounted for 57.1 percent of bad bot traffic in 2020. These are plaguing websites and often avoid detection by cycling through random IP addresses, entering through anonymous proxies, changing their identities, and mimicking human behavior.

> Bad bots have taken a liking to mobile identities. While Chrome remains a favorite identity for bad bots to impersonate, its overall share significantly dropped in 2020. Mobile clients like Mobile Safari, Mobile Chrome and others accounted for 28.1 percent of all bad bot requests in 2020. This is a significant increase compared to last year's 12.9 percent.[11]

That the Russians routinely attempt to manipulate American public opinion, even on healthcare matters, is beyond dispute. A team of researchers led by George Washington University's David A. Broniatowski, published an abstract titled, *Weaponized Health Communication: Twitter Bots and Russian Trolls Amplify the Vaccine Debate.* The National Institutes of Health article revealed that *the*

---

[10] Ezer Hasson, "Bad Bot Report 2021: The Pandemic of the Internet," 13 April 2021; https://www.imperva.com/blog/bad-bot-report-2021-the-pandemic-of-the-internet/

[11] Ibid. Hasson adds: Bad bots interact with applications in the same way a legitimate user would, making them harder to detect and prevent. They enable high-speed abuse, misuse, and attacks on websites, mobile apps, and APIs. They allow bot operators, attackers, unsavory competitors, and fraudsters to perform a wide array of malicious activities. Such activities include web scraping, competitive data mining, personal and financial data harvesting, brute-force login, digital ad fraud, spam, transaction fraud, and more.

Russians will take both sides of an issue for the purpose of misleading and dividing public opinion. For example, in debates such as the use of COVID-19 vaccines.

Results: Compared with average users, Russian trolls ($\chi^2(1)$ = 102.0; P < .001), sophisticated bots ($\chi^2(1)$ = 28.6; P < .001), and "content polluters" (χ^2 (1) = 7.0; P < .001) tweeted about vaccination at higher rates. Whereas content polluters posted more antivaccine content ($\chi^2(1)$ = 11.18; P < .001), Russian trolls amplified both sides. Unidentifiable accounts were more polarized ($\chi^2(1)$ = 12.1; P < .001) and antivaccine ($\chi^2(1)$ = 35.9; P < .001). *Analysis of the Russian troll hashtag showed that its messages were more political and divisive.*

Conclusions: Whereas bots that spread malware and unsolicited content disseminated antivaccine messages, *Russian trolls promoted discord.* Accounts masquerading as legitimate users create false equivalency, eroding public consensus on vaccination. Public Health Implications. Directly confronting vaccine skeptics enables bots to legitimize the vaccine debate. More research is needed to determine how best to combat bot-driven content.[12]

While iconic Lenin has faded from Russian public view, the conspiratorial nature of the state he founded in 1917 remains. In contrast to the social democracy postulated by Karl Marx, the Leninist state is autocratic. Russian state power today is concentrated in the hands of Vladimir Putin and his coterie of friends in the security services and big business. The offensive against Western democracies launched by the Cheka in the 1920s merely passed to the SVR. All that has changed is the technology and operational methods used, not the political aim.

---

[12] Abstract, "Weaponized Health Communication: Twitter Bots and Russian Trolls Amplify the Vaccine Debate," David A. Broniatowski, Ph.D., et.al. Broniatowski is a George Washington University professor and Associate Director of the Institute for Data, Democracy and Politics in the School of Engineering and Applied Science. The article and others like it may be found in the National Institutes of Health website. Italics have been added for emphasis.

Print is the sharpest and strongest weapon of our Party.

J.V. Stalin

Agitation for the masses; propaganda for the few.

V.I. Lenin

CHAPTER 9

BOTS AND TROLLS, SPIES AND CASE OFFICERS

*It seems to me proper now to treat of conspiracies, being a matter of
so much danger both to princes and to subjects; for history teaches us
that many more princes have lost their lives and their states by
conspiracies than by open war.*

Niccolo Machiavelli

From the 1920s to the end of the Soviet Union in 1991, Soviet
intelligence operatives were constantly on the lookout for individuals
of other nationalities—especially Americans—who could become
agents of influence. These people would have no overt tie to Russia
or the world Communist movement but would serve the Party's end
by writing, speaking, voting, or taking some other action as directed
by The Center.[1] The KGB and the Soviet Union are gone, but the
SVR has taken over the KGB's foreign disinformation duties, albeit
without Communist jargon. Its sister service, the GRU, is no less
active in its covert attacks on the West, specifically America.

INTELLIGENCE OFFICERS

The most traditional influencer is an intelligence officer, or
case officer, who specializes in covert influence operations. Case
officers supervise and direct illicit sources—agents, AKA spies.
Specialists in influencing foreign groups are known as Covert Action
(CA) operations officers. Covert Action can be defined as *"the
implementation of a nation's foreign policy through intelligence means."*[2]

A CA ops officer operates secretly through agents of influence—
spies under his control—who are in a position to shape public

---

[1] "The Center" is the term used by Russian intelligence to denote the old Lubyanka
headquarters of the KGB or Yasenovo, the new headquarters of its descendent, the SVR.

[2] Author's definition.

opinion, but whose connection to the case officer remains hidden. Typically, a Russian CA ops officer provides guidance to agents concerning a general line or theme to place in Western media. They may even convey a specific message that The Center wishes to appear. The agent is left to use his or her contacts in the media or influential organizations to float the desired theme or message.

In these Covert Action operations, the Russian government supplies a case officer with material that may run the gamut from denigrating an adversary, endorsing policy positions, or pretending to represent or promote the view of some third group. The case officer may even be called upon to present himself as something he is not. He would assume a public persona undercover, quite apart from his true intelligence affiliation.

The Great Powers have used agents of influence—spies—for several centuries to urge or coerce adversary governments to modify foreign policies favorable to the Covert Action operation. The Russians have long considered active measures, "*aktivnoye meropriyatiye*," an integral mechanism for achieving foreign policy goals. In some cases, Russian Covert Action takes precedence over normal diplomacy.

Veteran Czech intelligence officer, Ladislav Bittman, noted that the Cheka's first major deception operation outside Russian borders was Operation Trust. Aimed at the émigré community and French and British governments between 1922 and 1927, the Cheka and its successor, the OGPU, constructed a phantom anti-Bolshevik movement[3] that supposedly operated inside the Soviet Union.

Western European intelligence services were led into operational involvement with Cheka officers masquerading as anti-regime activists.[4] Cheka operatives abroad then played the role of members and supporters of the phantom organization with the objective of luring émigrés to Russia where they were promptly arrested and shot.[5]

---

[3] Known as "The Trust," a fictitious Tsarist shadow government supposedly poised to oust the Bolsheviks.

[4] Ladislav Bittman, op.cit, p.36. Bittman specialized in covert influence operations directed against the West from 1954 to 1968 when the Russians invaded Czechoslovakia.

[5] Bittman, op.cit., p. 36

Bittman gives a vivid example of the influence operation which he himself helped design and run, at Soviet behest, to convince Western audiences that Nazi groups were active in West Germany in the late 1950s. The ruse was widely believed until the Soviet invasion of Czechoslovakia in August 1968 when the true nature of the operation was revealed.

Czechoslovak intelligence was behind extensive anti-American, anti-British, and anti-French campaigns in West Germany in the name of a nonexistent, pro-Nazi organization known as *Kampfverband für Unabhaengiges Deutschland* (Fighting Group for Independent Germany). Fascist proclamations and threatening letters against allied units in West Germany were mailed to American, British, and French diplomats and to officers and soldiers stationed there.[6]

JOURNALIST AGENTS

Well-placed journalists are of particular interest to Russian intelligence officers. Such individuals have professional access to people of influence, such as government officials. Journalists can become sources of privileged information, and they also have the ability to place their own messages, or those of The Center, in the mass media. Hence, Russia began posing its agents and spies as journalists around the world.

In his testimony before the Permanent Select Committee on Intelligence, House of Representatives, in July 1982, Stanislav Levchenko, a former KGB officer and specialist for active measures, confirmed that the KGB gives major attention to foreign journalists by classifying them as permanent targets. When Levchenko was assigned to

---

[6] Bittman, op.cit. pp. 38-39; this operation was designed to raise doubts about the West German government and, if possible, delay the rearmament of the West German Bundeswehr.

Japan in 1974 as a field case officer, he was first required
to work a year with the Soviet magazine New Times, to
improve his journalistic skills. At the time, the magazine
employed twelve full-time correspondents abroad, of which
ten were KGB operatives. The KGB station in Japan,
where Levchenko operated from 1975 until he defected in
1979, handled more than two hundred agents, including
members of the Japanese parliament, prominent members
of the Japanese Socialist party, scientists, and journalists.
Levchenko himself handled ten agents and confidential
contacts, of whom four were journalists. One of his agents
was a close confidant of the owner of a major Japanese
newspaper with a circulation of more than three million
copies.[7]

TROLLS AND BOTS—THE NEW CASE OFFICERS

Since the 1990s and advances in artificial intelligence (AI),
old-line covert action officers are sharing the stage with artificial
beings of the bot family. It may be that traditional agent of influence
operations are gradually giving way to operations dependent upon
computer technology. In their methods and effects, trolls, bots, and
case officers are similar. Their operational purpose is the same—to
influence foreign audiences and governments to act in ways directed
by The Center. A technically trained case officer, known as a TOPS
or tech-ops officer, could serve as a troll while also being a case
officer handling agents of influence, especially other trolls.

A paper by Cornell University researcher, Terrence Adams,
makes the following observation about how advances in AI in the
not-distant future could easily substitute humans in the process of
persuasion:

This paper gives an overview of impersonation bots that
generate output in one, or possibly, multiple modalities. We

---

[7] Ladislav Bittman, The KGB and Soviet Disinformation: An Insider's View, pp. 77-78

also discuss rapidly advancing areas of machine learning and artificial intelligence that could lead to frighteningly powerful new multi-modal social bots. Our main conclusion is that most commonly known bots are one dimensional (i.e., chatterbot), and far from deceiving serious interrogators. However, using recent advances in machine learning, it is possible to unleash incredibly powerful, human-like armies of social bots, in potentially well coordinated campaigns of deception and influence.[8]

Technical details of how bots actually work are best known to computer specialists, but we can mention several members of the bot family which have niche functions.

Destructive bots are considered malware or malicious software.

Spambots roam the Internet vacuuming up e-mail addresses to sell to commercial entities or an intelligence service. A hostile intelligence service could use spambots to tap into personal or corporate electronic correspondence.

Botnets or teams of bots are capable of spreading viruses and rendering a network useless or compromised.

Along with bots is the use of AI to create an image of a person or place which is altered or completely fictitious. New technology is capable of making such misrepresentation appear perfectly genuine. This gives Russian covert influence operatives greatly improved capabilities to present credible, but manufactured, images to uninformed—or predisposed—audiences.

Perhaps pioneered by the movie industry, two related artificial technologies are now available for use in disinformation: Deep Fake Technology and its sister, Deep Video Portrait. In former days, the Soviet airbrush could make politically inconvenient people disappear from photographs. Crude splicing could also make foreign dignitaries appear to be doing dishonorable things or conferring with disreputable people.

---

[8] Terrence Adams, "AI-Powered Social Bots," 16 June 2017; https://arxiv.org/pdf/1706.05143.pdf

SLEEPER BOTS

We must glance back to the scenario outlined for us by PLA colonels Qiao Liang and Wang Xiangsui. If the Russians have read Chinese military writings, they must have absorbed some points of "Unrestricted Warfare" and adapted them to their own needs. The release by either China or Russia of armies of bots into Western Internet systems could bring about the effects described by Qiao Liang and Wang Xiangsui as the "Battlefield Beyond the Battlefield."

If the Russians have taken a leaf from Qiao and Wang, it seems probable that the Internet Research Agency has already quietly inserted parts of itself into many networks, public and private, but left those networks otherwise untouched for the moment. Qiao and Wang refer to burying "*a computer virus and hacker detachment in the opponent's computer system in advance.*" They probably are referring to swarms of botnets. In theory, a network hit by botnets could be put out of operation in a matter of minutes.

The use of "sleeper agents" is a method as old as spycraft. There is no reason why "sleeper bots" or logic bombs cannot remain at rest for years before they are awakened—activated—by an SVR officer in Moscow. Alternatively, botnets might be used to capture a computer network and bring it under an adversary's control. Obviously, men with a deep and rich sense of humor, PLA Colonels Qiao Liang and Wang Xiangsui have humorously described the ideal valorous soldier of the People's Liberation Army of the future:

> The era of "strong and brave soldiers who are heroic defenders of the nation" has already passed. In a world where even "nuclear warfare" will perhaps become obsolete military jargon, it is likely that a pasty-faced scholar wearing thick eyeglasses is better suited to be a modern soldier than is a strong young lowbrow with bulging biceps.[9]

---

[9] Qiao and Wang, op.cit., p. 44

The point the "jolly" colonels made is that the nature of warfare has fundamentally changed, and that brainpower applied to 21st-century high technology has moved to center stage. We might note some dark humor of our own: *"No danger is greater than a high IQ with evil intentions."* Neither the Chinese nor the Russians will leave any opportunity untouched if it has the least chance of setting Americans at each other's throats.

> *Hee was carefull and liberall to obtaine good intelligence from all parts abroad. Hee had such Moles perpetually working and casting to undermine him.*[10]

Sir Francis Bacon

---

[10] *History of the Reign of King Henry VII* (1622)

CHAPTER 10

RUSSIA'S HACKING OPERATIONS

*The rapid growth of computer technology offers perpetrators of
Communist disinformation opportunities totally unknown several
years ago. If a few bright American high school students can break
computer codes and manipulate sophisticated business and university
computers, professionally trained KGB operatives and computer
specialists can accomplish the same feat. Extracting valuable intelligence
from a computer or feeding a computer network with skillfully designed
disinformation creates a new challenge.*[1]

Ladislav Bittman

Given vast new opportunities to pillage and despoil the United
States, made possible through the miracle of technology, the Russians
embarked on their most daring operation around 2014—the capture
of state power of their main enemy. Their specific operational aim
was to use the new means of warfare at hand to shape the American
national political situation to their liking. The Russians knew they
were playing for high stakes by employing active measures to
influence the outcome of America's national election in 2016.

Through cleverly managed influence operations, Russian
intelligence hacked and manipulated the U.S. Presidential Election
of 2016, and to some extent the election of 2020. Much evidence of
the manipulation remains classified, but the Mueller investigations
give us a glimpse into Russian interference.

Drawing upon their experiences within the U.S. Intelligence
Community, Generals Michael Hayden and James Clapper
penned an open letter that was published November 10, 2021, in
the Washington Post.

---

[1] Ladislav Bittman, The KGB and Soviet Disinformation: An Insider's View; p. 66

We have personally seen the lengths to which our foreign adversaries will go to take advantage of any cracks in the foundation of our democracy. One of us was director of national intelligence during the period leading up to the 2016 presidential vote and saw firsthand how Russia used social media to exploit disinformation, polarization and divisiveness. The Russians' objective was to breed discord, and they succeeded beyond their wildest expectations. Now others have gone to school on the Russian example and will seek to prey on our country's state of affairs in just the same way.

Unfortunately, adversaries are finding increasingly fertile ground for their efforts. A society struggling to separate fact from fiction is the perfect environment for these actors to further erode electoral trust and kick democracy into a death spiral.[2]

Clapper and Hayden believe that further such manipulation and interference is highly likely until technical and procedural changes are made which limit Russian and Chinese intrusion into the American electoral process. They cite the Capitol rioting of January 6, 2021, and the resignation of experienced election officers facing threats of violence from American extremists. This all happened, at least in part, due to subtle Sino-Russian attacks on the American electoral system.

In the wake of the Election of 2016, in which Russian influence of the Trump campaign became obvious, pressure built for the appointment of a Special Counsel within the Department of Justice to investigate allegations of manipulation and collusion. A distinguished attorney, Robert S. Mueller III, was appointed to conduct a thorough investigation into the allegations. The product of his research was a lengthy and detailed report titled, "Report on

---

[2] James R. Clapper and Michael Hayden "Opinion: We must protect our elections now. National security is at stake." Washington Post, 10 November 2021; www.washingtonpost.com/opinion/2021/11/10/clapper-hayden-national-security-elections-integrity-letter

the Investigation into Russian Interference in the 2016 Presidential Election," which was issued in two volumes in March 2019.

Although it is extensively redacted for privacy and national security reasons, the Mueller report nevertheless lays bare the technical expertise, broad extent, and utter ruthlessness of the Russian political warfare offensive against the United States.

The report is so rich with detail, covering not only the information warfare objectives of the Russians but the technical means for achieving their ends, that extensive quotation from the Mueller report is fully merited. The following excerpt is from Volume I, Section 2:

RUSSIAN HACKING OPERATIONS[3]

At the same time that the IRA [ed. Internet Research Agency] operation began to focus on supporting candidate Trump in early 2016, the Russian government employed a second form of interference: cyber intrusions (hacking) and releases of hacked materials damaging to the Clinton Campaign. The Russian intelligence service known as the Main Intelligence Directorate of the General Staff of the Russian Army (GRU)[4] carried out these operations.

In March 2016, the GRU began hacking the email accounts of Clinton Campaign volunteers and employees, including campaign chairman John Podesta. In April 2016, the GRU hacked into the computer networks of the Democratic Congressional Campaign Committee (DCCC) and the Democratic National Committee (DNC). The GRU stole hundreds of thousands of documents from the compromised email accounts and networks. Around the time that the DNC announced in mid-June 2016 the Russian government's role in hacking its network, the GRU began dissemi-

---

[3] Robert S. Mueller III, "Report on the Investigation Into Russian Interference in the 2016 Presidential Election;" Volume I; Washington, D.C.; March 2019

[4] GRU: Glavnoye Razvedivetelnoye Upravleniye in Russian or "Main Intelligence Directorate." This organization recruits foreigners and carries out paramilitary operations such as those conducted in Crimea in 2014. It is subordinate to the Russian General Staff.

nating stolen materials through the fictitious online personas "DCLeaks" and "Guccifer 2.0." The GRU later released additional materials through the organization WikiLeaks.

The presidential campaign of Donald J. Trump ("Trump Campaign" or "Campaign") showed interest in WikiLeaks's releases of documents and welcomed their potential to damage candidate Clinton. Beginning in June 2016, SEC-TION REDACTED forecast to senior Campaign officials that WikiLeaks would release information damaging to candidate Clinton. WikiLeaks's first release came in July 2016. Around the same time, candidate Trump announced that he hoped Russia would recover emails described as missing from a private server used by Clinton when she was Secretary of State (he later said that he was speaking sarcastically). SECTION REDACTED WikiLeaks began releasing Podesta's stolen emails on October 7, 2016, less than one hour after a U.S. media outlet released video considered damaging to candidate Trump. Section III of this Report details the Office's investigation into the Russian hacking operations, as well as other efforts by Trump Campaign supporters to obtain Clinton-related emails.

The foregoing excerpt amply describes the techniques employed by Russian intelligence—in this case, the GRU. On one hand, the Internet Research Agency, here clearly acting under the operational guidance of the GRU, placed a series of messages on American social media supportive of candidate Trump as early as fall 2015 and into spring 2016. The Russians assessed that Trump as president would be more favorable to their interests.

In March 2016, aggressive hacking followed, which succeeded in breaking into the Democratic National Committee's computer networks. Some information was stolen and other information was altered or corrupted. The DNC evidently realized only in June 2016 what was taking place. By that time, the Russians had begun planting stolen information into social media channels and eventually through Julian Assange's WikiLeaks. WikiLeaks is an ideal platform for SVR or GRU dissemination of gray source influence material. Summer 2016 was the perfect time for revelations posted by such sources as DCLeaks, Guccifer 2.0, and WikiLeaks. Arguably, the great majority of American voters paid little if any attention to these or similar sources of information, but several million Americans did pay attention and accepted, either wholly or in part, what they read. These individuals served as key communicators to groups they were affiliated with.

The findings of the investigative team within the Department of Justice concluded the following:[5]

> First, the Office determined that Russia's two principal in-
> terference operations in the 2016 U.S. presidential election—
> the social media campaign and the hacking-and-dumping
> operations— violated U.S. criminal law. Many of the
> individuals and entities involved in the social media cam-
> paign have been charged with participating in a conspiracy
> to defraud the United States by undermining through
> deceptive acts the work of federal agencies charged with
> regulating foreign influence in U.S. elections, as well as
> related counts of identity theft. See United States v. Internet
> Research Agency, et al., No. 18-cr-32 (D.D.C.). Separately,
> Russian intelligence officers who carried out the hacking
> into Democratic Party computers and the personal email
> accounts of individuals affiliated with the Clinton Cam-
> paign conspired to violate, among other federal laws, the
> federal computer-intrusion statute, and they have been so
> charged. See United States v. Netyksho, et al., No. 18-cr-
> 215 (D.D.C.). SECTION REDACTED.

---

[5] Mueller, op.cit.

SOWING SEEDS OF DISCORD AND DIVISION

Technical prowess in intercepting private e-mails and documents is only part of the operational picture. An influence operation, certainly one as sophisticated as the Russians are capable of orchestrating, also involves contact with people. Case officers specialize in dealing with people.

RUSSIAN CONTACTS WITH THE CAMPAIGN[6]

The social media campaign and the GRU hacking operations coincided with a series of contacts between Trump Campaign officials and individuals with ties to the Russian government. The Office investigated whether those contacts reflected or resulted in the Campaign conspiring or coordinating with Russia in its election-interference activities. Although the investigation established that the Russian government perceived it would benefit from a Trump presidency and worked to secure that outcome, and that the Campaign expected it would benefit electorally from information stolen and released through Russian efforts, the investigation did not establish that members of the Trump Campaign conspired or coordinated with the Russian government in its election interference activities. The Russian contacts consisted of business connections, offers of assistance to the Campaign, invitations for candidate Trump and Putin to meet in person, invitations for Campaign officials and representatives of the Russian government to meet, and policy positions seeking improved U.S.-Russian relations.[7]

Nicely complementing social media disinformation campaigns and computer hacking, the Russians carefully orchestrated contacts between their case officers and diplomats with key members of the

---

[6] Mueller, op.cit.

[7] Mueller, op.cit.

Trump Campaign. The Russians made no secret of their wish to see candidate Trump elected and made several offers of assistance.

Russian ambassador Sergei Kislyak played a part in this orchestrated influence campaign, but so did a number of shadowy, lesser-known individuals. Three examples are all that are necessary to show the expertise of the GRU in conducting their well-planned influence campaign.

The Russians may initially have thought their ties with Carter Page, a pro-Russian foreign policy adviser to the Trump campaign, would be useful; however, the campaign quietly dropped Page in late September. Perhaps the Trump team viewed Page as a political liability, but it may also be that the Russians had second thoughts that having someone like Page—with his obviously pro-Russian views—did not serve their interests in seeing Trump elected.

In July 2016, Campaign foreign policy advisor Carter Page traveled in his personal capacity to Moscow and gave the keynote address at the New Economic School. Page had lived and worked in Russia between 2003 and 2007. After returning to the United States, Page became acquainted with at least two Russian intelligence officers, one of whom was later charged in 2015 with conspiracy to act as an unregistered agent of Russia. Page's July 2016 trip to Moscow and his advocacy for pro-Russian foreign policy drew media attention. The Campaign then distanced itself from Page and, by late September 2016, removed him from the Campaign.[8]

Campaign chairman Paul Manafort, a close adviser to candidate Trump, met with a suspected Russian case officer, Konstantin Kilimnik, ostensibly to discuss a peace plan involving Ukraine that Kilimnik claimed had the approval of the highest levels of the Russian government.

---

[8] Mueller, op.cit.

Separately, on August 2, 2016, Trump campaign chairman Paul Manafort met in New York City with his long-time business associate Konstantin Kilimnik, who the FBI assesses to have ties to Russian intelligence. Kilimnik requested the meeting to deliver in person a peace plan for Ukraine that Manafort acknowledged to the Special Counsel's Office was a "backdoor" way for Russia to control part of eastern Ukraine; both men believed the plan would require candidate Trump's assent to succeed (were he to be elected President). They also discussed the status of SECTION REDACTED Trump Campaign and Manafort's strategy for winning Democratic votes in Midwestern states. Months before that meeting, Manafort had caused internal polling data to be shared with Kilimnik, and the sharing continued for some period of time after their August meeting.[9]

Rounding out the selected examples presented is the late December request made by former National Security Adviser, Michael Flynn, who asked Ambassador Kislyak to cable Vladimir Putin requesting Russia not retaliate against American moves.

On December 29, 2016, then-President Obama imposed sanctions on Russia for having interfered in the election. Incoming National Security Advisor Michael Flynn called Russian Ambassador Sergey Kislyak and asked Russia not to escalate the situation in response to the sanctions. The following day, Putin announced that Russia would not take retaliatory measures in response to the sanctions at that time. Hours later, President-Elect Trump tweeted, "Great move on delay (by V. Putin)." The next day, on December 31, 2016, Kislyak called Flynn and told him the request had been received at the highest levels and Russia had chosen not to retaliate as a result of Flynn's request.[10]

---

[9] Mueller, op.cit.

[10] Mueller, op.cit.

Russian intelligence clearly has the ability to manipulate American public opinion, obstruct Constitutional processes, and even interpose its will on American foreign policy. Russia's well-crafted influence campaign, begun perhaps in late 2015, paid handsome dividends by late 2016.

Before moving off the subject of Russian covert political influence, perhaps one more point is worth making. To give credit where credit is due, the Russians did their homework in assessing many of America's target audiences. It is a fair guess that at the Internet Research Agency's headquarters there are target studies on practically every major group—ethnic, religious, occupational, educational, or regional. Hours of careful study and much thought went into the crafting of the covert campaign of 2015-2016. Well before the first social media post, the Russians knew exactly what they wanted and expected from each American target audience. For the most part, they were not disappointed.

The Russians fully expected that Americans who live on social media would be their most useful helpers in spreading the word. They also knew that Americans, by and large, are not critical thinkers and that many would accept at face value whatever they saw on social media. In this judgment, the Russians were not mistaken.

Leaving American gullibility aside, the point remains that the Russians did, with malicious intent to deceive, plant false and misleading information in order to divide us and sow hatred and enmity among the American people. We Americans merely helped them do it.

II. RUSSIAN "ACTIVE MEASURES" SOCIAL MEDIA CAMPAIGN[11]

The first form of Russian election influence came principally from the Internet Research Agency, LLC (IRA), a Russian organization funded by Yevgeniy Viktorovich Prigozhin and companies he controlled, including Concord Management and Consulting LLC and Concord Catering (collectively

---

[11] Mueller, op.cit.

"Concord.") The IRA conducted social media operations targeted at large U.S. audiences with the goal of sowing discord in the U.S. political system. These operations constituted "active measures" . . . a term that typically refers to operations conducted by Russian security services aimed at influencing the course of international affairs.

The IRA and its employees began operations targeting the United States as early as 2014. Using fictitious U.S. personas, IRA employees operated social media accounts and group pages designed to attract U.S. audiences. These groups and accounts, which addressed divisive U.S. political and social issues, falsely claimed to be controlled by U.S. activists. Over time, these social media accounts became a means to reach large U.S. audiences. IRA employees traveled to the United States in mid-2014 on an intelligence-gathering mission to obtain information and photographs for use in their social media posts.

IRA employees posted derogatory information about a number of candidates in the 2016 U.S. presidential election. By early to mid-2016, IRA operations included supporting the Trump Campaign and disparaging candidate Hillary Clinton. The IRA made various expenditures to carry out those activities, including buying political advertisements on social media in the names of U.S. persons and entities. Some IRA employees, posing as U.S. persons and without revealing their Russian association, communicated electronically with individuals associated with the Trump Campaign and with other political activists to seek to coordinate political activities, including the staging of political rallies. The investigation did not identify evidence that any U.S. persons knowingly or intentionally coordinated with the IRA's interference operation.

By the end of the 2016 U.S. election, the IRA had the ability to reach millions of U.S. persons through their social media accounts.[12]

America will hold its next national election in November 2024. From the Russian perspective, who the candidates will be is almost irrelevant in terms of personality or party affiliation. The central question determining how the Russians will attempt to intervene is this: "*Which candidate is more likely to serve our interest in dividing and agitating the American people?*" It is beyond question that the Internet Research Agency—the GRU and SVR—will attempt to work their will, assisted by a motley gaggle of "useful idiots" and extremists enlisted from the disaffected American fringe.

Have we learned from the divisive experiences of the past several years? Do we recognize the price of Russian meddling? How will the American people deal with future assaults on their Constitutional system? These are the questions we must ask ourselves moving forward.

Divide and rule.
"Divide et impera."

Julius Caesar

---

[12] Mueller, op.cit.

PART FIVE

WREAKING HAVOC

CHAPTER 11

MANIPULATING TRUE BELIEVERS

It is the true believer's ability to "shut his eyes and stop his ears"
to facts that do not deserve to be either seen or heard which is the
source of his unequaled fortitude and constancy. He cannot be
frightened by danger or disheartened by obstacles nor baffled by
contradictions because he denies their existence. Strength of faith,
as Bergson points out, manifests itself not in moving mountains but
in not seeing mountains to move. And it is the certitude of his infallible
doctrine that renders the true believer impervious to the uncertainties,
surprises and the unpleasant realities of the world around him.[1]

Eric Hoffer

It is far easier for a skilled propagandist to devise a line of persuasion for those holding fixed beliefs than it is for others who are skeptical of all information, willing to consider alternatives, open to receiving ideas and information that may contrast with their own tentative opinions.

From his experience as a Czech covert influence officer, often acting at the behest of the Russians, Ladislav Bittman made the following observation about the credulity of true believers:

What makes the disinformation message credible and acceptable even if the source is anonymous or unreliable? Most disinformation clearly serves the receiver's [ed. target's] needs by playing upon his prejudice and bias. . . . Extremists on each end of the political spectrum, left or right, are usually the easiest targets for deception. Without a healthy degree of tolerance and skepticism, they [ed. the extremists] tend to accept even bizarre accusations

---

[1] Eric Hoffer, The True Believer: Thoughts on the Nature of Mass Movements; 1951, p.79

and reports of conspiracy reaching them from unreliable sources if the messages are tuned to their political bias.[2]

Believers holding rigid views are susceptible to deception precisely because of their fixed views and inability to question their own beliefs. Such individuals do not seek alternative views, information that conflicts with their views, or even dialog with persons holding other views. Rather, true believers seek information confirming the truth of their existing beliefs. In effect, the true believer is incapable of seeing any "truth" but his own and is therefore self-propagandizing.

As Bittman noted, *"disinformation clearly serves the receiver's needs by playing upon his prejudice and bias."* More broadly, but substantially in accord with Bittman, Jacques Ellul explains why propaganda can be effective with the target audiences for whom it is formulated:

> An analysis of propaganda therefore shows that it succeeds primarily because it corresponds exactly to a need of the masses. Let us remember just two aspects of this: the need for explanations and the need for values, which both spring largely, though not entirely, from the promulgation of the news.[3]

Across many centuries people have shown themselves willing to kill or die for what they believe. "Wars of belief" mar the pages of history. Perhaps no wars are as savage and pitiless as those fought between opposing belief systems—religions or ideologies.

CONFIRMATION BIAS

University of Chicago Professor Jane L. Risen's theoretical research into belief formation dovetails well with Jacques Ellul's practical observations on the effectiveness of well-crafted propaganda. Citing thirteen authorities, Risen describes human thought processes

---

[2] Bittman, The KGB and Soviet Disinformation: An Insider's View, p. 56

[3] Jacques Ellul, Propaganda: The Formation of Men's Attitudes; 1965, p. 146

as having two components, described as System One and System Two. The first is intuitive and automatic. The second is deliberative.

> . . . each of these accounts involves the idea that there is one set of mental processes that operates quickly and effortlessly and another [set] that operates in a deliberate and effortful manner. The quick and effortless set of mental processes is often referred to simply as "System 1" and the slow, deliberate set of processes is known as "System 2" (Stanovich & West, 2002).[4]

We might think of System One as the "snap judgment" often made when encountering an unfamiliar situation or person. An intuitive, instantaneous appraisal may have three components. The mind immediately reacts with a "*this seems like . . .*" or superficial categorization of the new situation, person, or thing compared to previous similar experiences.

The second component is the mind's automatic construction of some causal explanation or meaning. This can lead to sometimes false connections being made on the spur of the moment. Later, it proves hard to erase constructed beliefs from the more deliberative side of the brain.

The third aspect is an unconscious search for evidence that appears to confirm the snap judgment. Our brains look for evidence to back up our initial experience, even if the judgment is wrong. In rational or scientific thinking, the method of testing hypotheses is an attempt to *disprove*, not to confirm, a judgment.

It is possible that System One has an inherently deceptive "lock-on, lock-out" mode of operation that can and often does overwhelm the slower, more deliberative System Two. Mobs may be particularly susceptible to acting upon impulsive System One thinking, which overrides a more analytical, evaluative, but unfortunately much tardier System Two.

---

[4] Jane L. Risen, "Believing What We Do Not Believe," Psychological Review; American Psychological Association 2016, Vol. 123, No. 2, 182–207; https://www.apa.org/pubs/journals/features/rev-0000017.pdf

The broader context in which an individual finds himself also plays a major role in belief formation. Fear and uncertainty in unsettled or dangerous situations appear to be components in switching on intense System One thinking. Being a member of an agitated or angry group may be another component.

Other early accounts of superstition focused on a motivational component. Malinowski (1948) saw uncertainty and fear as primary motivators, arguing that the primary purpose of superstitious behavior is to reduce the tension associated with uncertainty and fill the void of the unknown. . . .

In contrast to uncertainty, which entails psychological costs, the feeling that one can understand, predict, and control one's environment confers psychological benefits (Thompson, 1981). Because superstitions can offer individuals a sense of understanding even when there is not sufficient information to develop an accurate causal explanation (Keinan, 1994), superstitions seem to be especially common when people are motivated to understand and control their environment. . . .

Furthermore, experiments that randomly assign participants to feel a lack of control find that they report more superstitious beliefs (Whitson & Galinsky, 2008). To be sure, exploration of people's limited cognition as well as the motivation to manage uncertainty contributes to our understanding of superstition. In particular, these accounts help explain why some populations exhibit more magical thinking than others as well as why magical thinking is especially likely to occur when experiencing uncertainty, stress, and anxiety.[5]

What Professor Risen tactfully calls "magical thinking" or superstition certainly applies to attempts by ancient peoples grasping

---

[5] Risen, op.cit.

for answers to questions about the physical world in which they lived. Magic seemed to be the only explanation of phenomena for which today we have scientific explanations.

Human beings of all ages needed explanations to help them cope with the changing seasons, bountiful or sparse harvests, birth and death, and many other questions. The most intelligent individuals usually ended up as the priests and prophets of ancient people. It is easy to understand how intelligent people could reach "explanations" by what today would be considered non-rational thought.

Professor Risen makes the point that it is not necessarily only people of low education and intelligence who fall into what she calls a confirmation bias trap, but upon occasion people of high intelligence, and presumably of some education, also fall into the very same cognitive trap of seeking only information that appears to confirm what they already believe.[6] Such confirmation merely strengthens their beliefs.

USING BELIEF AS A FOUNDATION FOR DECEPTION

Deception operations designed to mislead an enemy are based on confirmation bias thinking, as the intended target readily takes aboard certain bits of information, but ignores other bits to his peril. This is the point at which carefully crafted propaganda enters the equation. Propaganda is intended to transform people's beliefs into certain specific actions directed by the propagandist. Propaganda can certainly persuade and direct on a rational, deliberative, System Two plane, but it is most powerful when taking advantage of System One types of impulsive, reactive thinking. Jacques Ellul states:

In the world of politics and economics, the same holds true. The news is only about trouble, danger, and problems.

---

[6] It must also be said, however, that intelligent and well educated people are much less likely for several reasons to accept pat answers from questionable sources. Intelligent persons in general are more skeptical about what they hear and see, they often ask more questions than do unintelligent people, and invariably they are curious about "why the way things are" and seek answers for themselves. This has certainly been the case since Copernicus and Galileo offered views of the solar system that contradicted Church dogma. Educational systems are designed to teach intelligent people how to think critically.

This gives man the notion that he lives in a terrible and frightening era, that he lives amid catastrophes in a world where everything threatens his safety. Man cannot stand this; he cannot live in an absurd and incoherent world . . . nor can he accept the idea that the problems, which sprout all around him, cannot be solved, or that he himself has no value as an individual and is subject to the turn of events. . . .

And the more complicated the problems are, the more simple the explanations must be; the more fragmented the canvas, the simpler the pattern; the more difficult the question, the more all-embracing the solution; the more menacing the reduction of his own worth, the greater the need for boosting his ego. All this propaganda—and only propaganda—can give him.[7]

And further:

The secret of propaganda success or failure is this: has it or has it not satisfied the unconscious need of the individual whom it addressed? No propaganda can have an effect unless it is needed, though the need may not be expressed as such but remain unconscious.[8]

Jacques Ellul has much to say about the power of propaganda when directed to audiences having been subjected to stressful conditions or experiencing the uncertainty and fears mentioned by Professor Risen. Ellul notes that propaganda will cause an individual or group to act when conditions are as Risen describes them, and the propaganda speaks directly to each member of the target audience.

---

[7] Jacques Ellul, Propaganda, p. 146

[8] Ibid., p. 139

Man will act when he feels that a certain result needs to be obtained and that the need is urgent. Advertising demonstrates it to him in the commercial domain; propaganda demonstrates it in politics. Finally, man will be helped in this progression to action by example, by similar action all around him. But such similar action would not come to his attention except through the intermediary of propaganda.[9]

Propaganda can make the individual feel the urgency, the necessity, of some action, its unique character. And at the same time propaganda shows him what to do. The individual who burns with desire for action but does not know what to do is a common type in our society. He wants to act for the sake of justice, peace, progress, but does not know how. If propaganda can show him this "how," it has won the game: action will surely follow.[10]

As mentioned by Professor Risen, confirmation bias may be at the core of an individual's search for an explanation. Scientists attempt to disprove what they tentatively hold to be true. Most human beings, however, seek only information which proves their views to be correct. This tendency locks out alternative explanations, especially information that contradicts their views. Demosthenes, in ancient Greece, spoke to this point when he observed: *"Nothing is easier than self-deceit. For what each man wishes, that he also believes to be true."*

A skilled propagandist takes a measure of his target audience through painstaking analysis well before crafting any messages intended to cause action to take place. Often it is the case that the propagandist will tell his audience what they already think they know.

Dr. Risen describes confirmation bias, especially biases leading to acceptance of misleading or even completely false information, as follows:

---

[9] Ellul, op.cit., p. 209

[10] Ibid., p. 209

Confirmation bias. Researchers who study judgment and decision making note that one of the most common and devastating biases that people must manage is the confirmation bias—the tendency to search for and favor evidence that supports current beliefs and ignore or dismiss evidence that does not (Klayman & Ha, 1987; Wason, 1966).

Although the confirmation bias can be exacerbated when people deliberately use a positive test strategy, the bias initially emerges because System 1 processing tends to be fast and associative. Indeed, one reason that people fall prey to the confirmation bias is that simply considering a hypothesis automatically makes information that is consistent with that hypothesis accessible (Kahneman, 2011, see also Gilbert, 1991).

When considering whether someone is shy, for example, information that is consistent with that possibility is likely to immediately jump to mind. Different information is likely to jump to mind, however, when considering whether that same person is outgoing (see Snyder & Swann, 1978). The Wason (1966) four-card selection task has been used to illustrate how intuitive confirmatory thinking is and how much more effort is required for disconfirmatory thinking.

Although the confirmation bias emerges when people are indifferent to the hypothesis (participants do not have a stake in whether the Wason card rule is true), several lines of research show that the bias becomes much more pronounced when people are motivated to believe the hypothesis under consideration (Dawson, Gilovich, & Regan, 2002; Gilovich, 1991). . . . The confirmation bias is useful for understanding why superstitious intuitions are maintained even though they are not true.[11]

---

[11] Risen, op.cit.

So what makes confirmation bias such a dangerous trigger mechanism for whipping groups and individuals into acts that, in a calmer and more rational situation, they would eschew? Psychologists Gordon Pennycook and David Rand found that persons who were more reflective were less susceptible to fake news than were persons who were less reflective. On the other hand, news which echoed a person's established political beliefs, even if false, was more likely to be accepted.

> More-reflective participants had a somewhat lower overall belief [in false or fake news] than less-reflective participants, whereas overall belief was higher for politically concordant headlines than for politically discordant headlines . . . [12]

They also note, however, that overconfidence—a person thinking he knows more about a subject than he really knows—renders an individual vulnerable to accepting a lie as the truth. Overconfidence results from confirmation of a deeply held belief which can be fed by a propagandist or deception artist.

> Research also shows that overconfidence may contribute to susceptibility to false information, perhaps because it stops people from slowing down and engaging in reflective reasoning.[13]

Pennycook and Rand also raise the issue of what might be termed herd mentality. In layman's terms, an individual accepts a particular view or piece of information because everyone else does. This tendency, as Ellul pointed out, gives added power to a well-crafted propaganda message. Ellul notes that a mob is merely a collection of individuals, but it takes on a character of its own.

---

[12] Gordon Pennycook and David G. Rand; "The Psychology of Fake News," Trends in Cognitive Sciences; May 2021; Vol. 25, No. 5

[13] Ibid.

Social media creates just such a herd, which, incidentally, may exist only artificially thanks to bots and trolls.

Sourcing of information also is key for both acceptance of incoming information and the establishment of its veracity. For example, the late Walter Cronkhite was considered an unimpeachable source of news and commentary. In print journalism, the New York Times tops all other periodicals for veracity. Credibility often, but not always, accompanies elite status according to Pennycook and Rand. The problem, however, is that individuals customarily turn to their favorite source of information, whether it be Fox News, MSNBC, the New York Times, or InfoWars. Individuals view their favorite sources as credible.

> The source is another important cue that may be used when evaluating news. Participants are more likely to believe information provided by people whom they view as being credible, and a large literature from political science has robustly demonstrated the impact of elite messaging, in particular, on public opinion. For example, attributing a false claim to President Trump increased Trump support- ers' belief in the claim while reducing Democrats' belief in the claim.[14]

IMPASSIONED PERSONALITIES

Rand and Pennycook posed two related rhetorical questions about the packaging of messages, whether or not those messages are false or true. "Does the design of social media platforms actively promote the spread of misinformation? For example, by inducing distraction and incentivizing or directing attention to factors other than veracity?"

Given the examples of people like Alex Jones of InfoWars, the answer appears to be an unqualified "yes" regarding social media. In historical examples before social media, the bombastic styles of

---

[14] Pennycook and Rand, op.cit.

Benito Mussolini or the histrionic anger of Adolf Hitler shaking his fist were indeed central elements of their ability to mesmerize millions of followers. In other words, the message does play a part, but perhaps it is the *packaging* of that message which is more persuasive.

> Finally, a salient feature of fake news headlines also seems to be that they are often emotionally evocative. That is, fake news is often geared toward provoking shock, fear, anger, or (more broadly) moral outrage. This is important because people who report experiencing more emotion (positive or negative) at the outset of the task are more likely to believe false (but not true) news; and instructing people to rely on emotion increases belief in false (but not true) headlines.[15]

The 20th century witnessed the often visceral stimulus-response impact of modern propagandists like Hitler or Mussolini who were quite capable of whipping massive audiences of devotees into a frenzy. A case in point is the 1922 March on Rome, which overthrew Italy's weak but functioning constitutional monarchy to establish a fascist dictatorship. The March on Rome rested on Mussolini's exhortations alone. He told the mob what it already knew—that Italy's problems were due to the parliamentary system, and that action was required to put things right and make Italy great again, as in the glory days of the Roman Empire. The message was clear: sweep away what exists and install strongman rule. Mussolini's charismatic delivery of the message whipped the mob into action.

This same danger exists today in the United States of America. Small, but determined extremist groups are committed to making fundamental changes in the government and society. While much of this hatred and discontent is homegrown, it cannot be denied that it is egged on by hostile forces abroad.

---

[15] Pennycook and Rand, op.cit.

*All this was inspired by the principle—which is quite true within itself—
that in the big lie there is always a certain force of credibility; because the
broad masses of a nation are always more easily corrupted in the deeper
strata of their emotional nature than consciously or voluntarily; and thus in
the primitive simplicity of their minds they more readily fall victims to the
big lie than the small lie, since they themselves often tell small lies in little
matters but would be ashamed to resort to large-scale falsehoods.*[16]

Adolf Hitler

---

[16] Mein Kampf, Vol. I, Ch. X

CHAPTER 12

THE FOOD OF FOOLS[1]

To be in possession of an absolute truth is to have a net of familiarity spread over the whole of eternity. There are no surprises and no unknowns. All questions have already been answered, all decisions made, all eventualities foreseen. The true believer is without wonder and hesitation. . . . The true believer is emboldened to attempt the unprecedented and the impossible not only because his doctrine gives him a sense of omnipotence but also because it gives him unqualified confidence in the future.[2]

Eric Hoffer

The Russians have a lengthy history of playing upon people's biases and prejudices. They are easily capable of motivating individuals and groups already holding views compatible with their own. They are also equally adept at manipulating individuals and groups whose views vary widely from theirs. To motivate the latter, SVR case officers are capable of making themselves over to be acceptable to opposition groups. Because the operational goal is to manipulate and motivate, the image a case officer must present and the messages he or she delivers must conform exactly to the beliefs and prejudices of the targeted individuals and groups.

An officer in this case acts very much like the old *agent provocateur* of Cheka and Okhrana days. It is very much like being an actor who plays a role so convincingly that he is accepted as being something which he is not. Russian operatives, especially those having foreign or mixed cultural backgrounds, such as famed GRU operative, Richard Sorge, or British traitor, Kim Philby, are especially well-suited for operational tasks of this nature.

---

[1] Excerpt from Jonathan Swift (1667-1745) – "'Tis an old maxim in the schools, That flattery's the food of fools."

[2] Eric Hoffer, The True Believer, p. 82

As mentioned, there is a highly important first step to take if such an operation is to be successful. That step is a painstaking analytical assessment of the targeted groups and individuals to be manipulated. Months of investigative work must be completed before an undercover officer is set in motion. The Russians do careful work choosing the groups they influence.

Psychological operations officers go to great lengths to spot useful groups. This is no less true of those engaged in commercial marketing as it is to those in covert, or overt, political influence. The methodology of analysis is very much the same. The only difference is the action-based outcome desired.

If influence operations are to be effective, the intelligence service or marketing agency must know in exquisite detail—not merely the group they are targeting and where they live, but how that group and its members think and act under specific conditions. Marketing firms spend much time collecting all manner of data on their potential customers. By the same token, foreign intelligence organizations collect extensive personal information through open and clandestine sources. In both commercial and political operations the work of bots, as well as information collected by traditional human sources, contribute to the growing knowledge of the target audience.

Case officers look for vulnerabilities, occasionally called handles, which can be exploited to gain control over individuals. In agent recruitment, examples of vulnerabilities may be the need for money, questionable personal behavior, career problems, a burning desire for revenge, and myriad other such handles. These handles enable a skilled officer to enlist his target as a recruited agent. A key such vulnerability is a fixed—extremist—view of the world.

Officers seeking to influence groups or masses of people look for susceptibilities for the same operational end. More often than not, Russian case officers will consider a group's hatreds, biases, and prejudices to be their handles.

Unfortunately, in the United States, it is not difficult to find people and groups in our open society with prejudices, grievances, biases, resentments, and hatred. Hatred is especially characteristic of white supremacists on one hand, and black radical activists on the other.[3] These hatreds may be, and likely are, deep-set beliefs perhaps formed in childhood.

The SVR officer does not care what a person believes. He only cares to clearly understand what the belief is, so he may carry out his operational assignment. Often, groups and the human beings who comprise them, hold a family of related beliefs beyond one simple racial or political prejudice. Echoing Bittman, extremist groups' views exceed mere opinions and are, in fact, deep-set beliefs—often prepared for violent action.[4]

INFLAMING PASSIONS

The Department of Homeland Security sought the indictment of Elena Alekseevna Khusyaynova, a staff member of Russia's Internet Research Agency. The criminal indictment against Ms. Khusyaynova on charges of conspiracy to defraud the United States reads as follows:

> "... members of the Conspiracy used social media and other internet platforms to inflame passions on a wide variety of topics, including immigration, gun control and the Second Amendment, the Confederate flag, race relations, LGBT issues, the Women's March and the NFL anthem debate. Members of the Conspiracy took advantage of specific events in the United States to anchor their themes, including the shootings of church members in Charleston, South Carolina, and the concert attendees in Las Vegas, Nevada; the Charlottesville "Unite the Right" rally and the associated violence; police shootings of African- American

---

[3] The "Proud Boys" and "Oath Keepers" are examples of the former; "Antifa" (Anti-fascist) of the latter.

[4] Ellul, op.cit., p. 209 footnote: "One must offer the individual a specific, clear, simple task to be undertaken at a given moment. From the moment propaganda succeeds in personalizing its appeal, the individual who feels concerned is placed in a situation that demands a decision." An example is an inflammatory speech by a demagogue that goads an excited mob into taking violent action.

men; as well as the personnel and policy decisions of the current U.S. administration.[5]

The indictment clearly shows what the Internet Research Agency (IRA) was attempting to do, at least in broad outline,[6] but a closer examination is in order. What must be understood is the variety of audiences and the issues that motivate each. Note, for example, that playing upon Second Amendment rights may appeal to gun-rights activists, but is at sharp variance with playing upon the same issue as perceived by families grieving those murdered in the shootings. *Yet Russian disinformation specialists routinely play upon both issues with each group, albeit through different channels.*

The point made is that the Russian intelligence services do not particularly care either about gun rights or those murdered. In playing upon these divisive issues with opposing audiences, the Russians fan hatred between key groups of the American people. The result is to weaken the United States internally. That is Russia's operational goal, pure and simple. China certainly concurs.

The Russians are interested in fomenting violent clashes between whites and blacks.[7] The issue of police brutality is a Russian favorite and is admirably tailored for Russian disinformation. Not only is it perfectly suited for driving yet another wedge between American groups, but it is also ideologically appealing as an example of the superiority of communistic and dictatorship societies over what they claim is a racist and decadent democratic society. Moreover, an added benefit for both the Russians and the Chinese is using stories of American police brutality and racial violence to "vaccinate" their own peoples against any desire for western or democratic freedom.

The one and only common thread between these divisive issues and the opposing audiences affected by them is that the Russians

---

[5] DHS, op.cit., p. 27; the indictment was handed down on 28 September 2018; see United States of America v. Elena Alekseevna Khusyaynova, Eastern District of Virginia. IRA was engaged in "Project Lakhta." It is highly doubtful that Khusyaynova, or any other of the Russians, will ever be brought to trial.

[6] See https://www.justice.gov/usao-edva/press-release/file/1102591/download which is the formal Complaint filed 28 September 2018 containing many operational details of interest.

[7] The Chinese are understandably more concerned with attacks upon Asian Americans.

carefully select the issues. They know all too well they could cause Americans to clash—hopefully violently—with other Americans by cleverly presenting the issues. As noted earlier there is nothing as savage as a war of belief. Meanwhile, the Russians themselves sit on the sidelines and smirk.

The Russians can exploit the criminal act of one police officer, such as Derek Chauvin, to persuade black Americans and liberal groups throughout the U.S. that all policemen are that way. This is the use of confirmation bias as people reach snap judgments based on limited data, proving what they already have come to believe.

As activism *against* the police increases, the anticipated reaction takes place among other Americans who adopt hardened positions opposing radical liberals and display *Back the Blue* signs. Domestic debate ensues which further polarizes the American people, absorbs much time and attention, and raises further enmity.

So, which position is the correct one? The Russians really do not care. By sowing discord and opening old wounds among American groups, by playing heavily on Americans' worst prejudices and beliefs, the SVR and its TOPS officers in the Internet Research Agency achieved their operational goal. They drove another nail into America's self-inflicted wound.

If the United States is convulsed by its own internal controversies and disturbances it is less able to exert its influence abroad to stymie Russian or Chinese moves in Asia, the Middle East, and Europe. Consumed with issues at home, the U.S. is also far less capable of defending itself. As you can see, low visibility active measures can achieve Russian and Chinese political objectives with no casualties and little expense.

"AND LEADS YOU TO BELIEVE A LIE"[8]

It may be that throughout the centuries, religious and messianic political leaders have sought new followers from among the common people around them. Ordinary people face a number of challenges

---

[8] Excerpt from a poem by William Blake (1757-1827) – "This life's dim windows of the soul; Distorts the heavens from pole to pole; And leads you to believe the lie, When you see with, *not through,* the eye."

in their lives, some on a daily basis, regarding even the acquisition of the bare necessities of life. Need is the master of action. The success of the Bolsheviks in 1917 may be ascribed to three needs that neither Kerensky nor the monarchists recognized: land, peace, and bread.

Leon Trotsky mused: *"Life is not an easy matter . . . You cannot live through it without falling into frustration and cynicism unless you have before you a great idea which raises you above personal misery, above weakness, above all kinds of perfidy and baseness."* Under certain conditions, vulnerable people can be seduced into organizations with "great ideas." People who are frustrated or have become cynical about institutions are susceptible to extremist religions or political creeds, such as Communism or Fascism.

We are mindful at this point of Eric Hoffer's observations concerning fanatics and their subject masses:

> There is an exhilaration and getting out of one's skin in both participants and spectators. It is possible that the frustrated are more responsive to the might and splendor of the mass than people who are self-sufficient. The desire to escape or camouflage their unsatisfactory selves develops in the frustrated a facility for pretending—for making a show—and also a readiness to identify themselves wholly with an imposing mass spectacle.[9]

All active mass movements strive, therefore, to interpose a fact-proof screen between the faithful and the realities of the world.[10]

Lenin, a master organizer, political thinker, and revolutionary, advocated "agitation for the masses, and propaganda for the few." He used published material for the educated intelligentsia. Lenin clearly distinguished between Russia's relatively small educated population which could be persuaded by print media, and the uneducated and semi-educated masses to be stirred to action through agitation:

---

[9] Hoffer, op.cit. p.68

[10] Hoffer, op.cit, p.79

The art of any propagandist and agitator consists in his ability to find the best means of influencing any given audience, by presenting a definite truth, in such a way as to make it most convincing, most easy to digest, most graphic, and most strongly impressive.[11]

Published propaganda from the Internet Research Agency (IRA) often comes in the form of social media. Homeland Security notes that in 2018, *"Twitter identified and released information from 3,814 IRA-linked Twitter accounts and stated that they believed that approximately 1.4 million people had been in contact with an IRA-controlled account.*[12] These accounts had posted nearly 176,000 tweets in the ten weeks prior to the 2016 presidential elections.[13]

What may be said about Russian influence activities is that their skills on an operational level appear superior to those of their Chinese counterparts. In terms of the overall sophistication of strategy, however, Moscow lags far behind Beijing.

We may speculate that the Russians and Chinese view contemporary American society, with its growing extreme polarity in politics and chaotic social divisions, with a certain warm satisfaction. Violent Leftist and Rightwing groups, such as white supremacist groups and agitators like those in Portland and Seattle, provide fertile ground for sharply divisive campaigns that can be organized and directed from the comfort of a computer room in Moscow, St. Petersburg, or Shanghai.

The ignorant man always adores what he cannot understand.[14]

Cesare Lombroso

---

[11] As translated by Dora Cox in Lenin Collected Works, p. 141

[12] DHS, op.cit. p. 23; See also "Update on Twitter's Review of the 2016 US Election." January 19, 2018. https://blog.twitter.com/en_us/topics/company/2018/2016-election-update.html.

[13] Ibid., p. 32

[14] *The Man of Genius*, Part III, Ch 3. Lombroso, a physician and criminologist, is considered to be the "Father of Criminology" (1836-1909)

CHAPTER 13

SOWING SEEDS OF DISCORD

*Let us not forget that revolutions are accomplished
through people, although they be nameless.*

Leon Trotsky

Lenin is said to have coined the phrase "useful idiot" to describe people who aided the Bolshevik cause out of enthusiasm or ignorance but were not Bolsheviks themselves. In the same way, extremists of either the Left or the Right admirably suit Moscow's purposes. All that is needed is a key communicator with a sizable audience through whom the Russians may feed their disinformation.

The Russian GRU intelligence services found a "useful idiot" in Alexander E. Jones, an American talk-show host. Jones has an explosive, bombastic style that both repulses and fascinates viewers. He perfectly fits Lenin's description of an agitator. The shock power of his statements and wild gesticulations make a striking impression on the System One thought processes of many thousands of people. The impact Jones makes on the minds of his followers neutralizes whatever System Two rational and deliberative thinking may have existed.

Alex Jones effectively provides lurid pseudo-explanations for various events such as the Sandy Hook school shooting, and the 9/11 terrorist attack. In fairness to Jones, many of the lies he passes along to his devoted followers spring from his own fertile imagination. Extremist followers look to him for information, which conforms largely to their existing beliefs. Jones provides simplistic, pat answers that fill a limited quest for explanations. To the extent that leaders meet the simplest of psychological needs for their audiences, they shape behavior. The extremist leader speaks, and followers obey.

In addition to his own creative lies and distortions, Alex Jones gladly purveys Russian-supplied information, as he did during the

2016 Presidential campaign. It is an incontrovertible fact that Jones used materials stolen by Russian intelligence services, and passed them on with colorful embellishments to thousands of listeners.

A recent PBS Frontline program the "United States of Conspiracy" centered mainly on Alex Jones. During the documentary, the question arose whether Jones actually believes the preposterous lies he spews. Whether he is a true believer or merely a hypocrite out to make money off his followers is not important. *What is significant is that a staggering number of Jones' followers believe everything he says.*

One fireman from North Carolina actually believed Jones' Pizzagate lie. The man got out his hunting rifle, drove up to Washington, D.C., and opened fire in a pizza restaurant, convinced that "they" (the pizza makers) were butchering little children in the basement. After all, he explained to the police, Jones had informed him that scandalous activities were routinely taking place in the pizza parlor.

Jones' program *InfoWars* purports to have the inside story on a variety of spectacular events, but his show blatantly intends to stir heated controversy rather than to educate or inform. Jones exults in whipping up an excited audience, often by his own bizarre antics—wildly yelling and weeping. The Russians, and almost certainly the Chinese as well, are fully aware of Jones' large following and his ability to convince people of the many "hidden evils" committed by the U.S. Government, leading public officials, or federal agencies.

As Jacques Ellul observed, propaganda's success or failure rests upon satisfying the unconscious needs of the masses of individuals to whom it is addressed. Disinformation satisfies those needs and is effective in mobilizing some of the least desirable elements in American society to violence. The evidence is clear that these groups are motivated to action by clever agitation. It is also apparent that our Russian adversaries, in particular, and to a lesser extent their Chinese partners, are capitalizing on fringe disaffection through people such as Alex Jones. The Sino-Russian goal is to promote an increasingly divided, discordant, and unstable America. Alex Jones and others like him are faithfully doing their part toward that end.

TURNING A PANDEMIC TO GOOD USE

In the closing months of 2019, a new, highly virulent form of SARS appeared in Wuhan, China, which has become known as COVID-19.[1] The origin of the virus and the date of its first appearance is in dispute. The Chinese Communist Party initially attempted to suppress all news of the outbreak, going so far as to arrest Dr. Li Wenliang on charges of spreading rumors.[2] Dr. Li had simply tried to alert professional colleagues to the dangers of the virus.

In January 2020, Chinese official news sources began issuing carefully-worded bulletins regarding COVID-19. The initial message touted by the Chinese pointed to a natural origin, namely among certain bats native to southwestern China, which were being sold as food, along with snakes, birds, and mammals, in a Wuhan wet market. Western officials suggested the possibility that a sample of C-19 had escaped from a P-4 biological research facility in Wuhan. The Chinese quickly denied the allegation. Shortly thereafter, the Chinese Foreign Ministry disseminated the view that U.S. Army researchers created COVID-19 and smuggled it into Wuhan where it was released.[3] To date, there has been no objective and complete inquiry into the origin and appearance of COVID-19, and it is unlikely that such an investigation will ever be made.

The Wuhan Institute of Virology (WIV), a possible source of the C-19 virus, was placed under the direct control of the People's Liberation Army and was closed to international visitors. The Chinese have consistently denied access to the facility and refuse all requests for an impartial investigation into the outbreak. In some cases, China has responded to such requests with trade embargoes.

---

[1] COVID-19 is caused by a coronavirus called SARS-CoV-2. On 11 February 2020 the World Health Organization announced an official name for the disease that is causing the 2019 novel coronavirus outbreak, first identified in Wuhan China. The new name of this disease is "coronavirus disease 2019," abbreviated as COVID-19.

[2] Dr. Li Wenliang subsequently died of COVID-19 on 7 February 2020, age 34.

[3] Zhao Lijian, Ministry of Foreign Affairs, Twitter post [@zlj517] 12 March 2020. Zhao referred to "U.S. soldiers" competing in an international military sports event as the vectors. China and Russia have for decades accused the U.S. of using biological weapons during the Korean War (1950-53).

China's official reaction has added fuel to the fires of suspicion. In mid-February, Chen Wei, a major general in the People's Liberation Army and a leading biological weapons expert at the Academy of Military Science, was appointed to take the helm at the WIV. In April, new rules were set in place for academic publications on COVID-19. In particular, studies of the origins of the novel coronavirus were to be subject to special scrutiny and official approval.[4]

In the grand scheme of things, the origin of the C-19 virus is irrelevant. What is significant is its biological, economic, and political impact. Those are clear to the international community.

COVID-19 has made a severe impact on human beings and health providers around the globe. The rapid spread of infection in the early months of the pandemic cost thousands of lives and dealt a heavy blow to the global economy. Governments everywhere found themselves unprepared for the onset of a worldwide pandemic.

As 2021 drew to a close, COVID-19 was still a mortal threat as the virus changed its structure to adapt to vaccines and other measures put in place to control it. Worldwide, approximately 265 million people have been infected, with 5.25 million succumbing to the virus. The countries most heavily hit are, in order: the United States, India, Brazil, the U.K., and Russia. Nearly 900,000 Americans have died due to COVID-19 to date.[5] These statistics focus on actual numbers, but smaller countries may have suffered proportionately higher casualties.

The political significance of COVID-19 is found in two areas: how the Chinese have used the virus to their advantage in Third World countries, and how they have exploited the issue to further fragment the American people. The Chinese provided millions of doses of their vaccines Sinovac and Sinopharm to Africa and Asia. The People's Republic of China has made excellent use of

---

[4] Jing-Bao Nie, "In the Shadow of Biological Warfare: Conspiracy Theories on the Origins of COVID-19 and Enhancing Global Governance of Biosafety as a Matter of Urgency," *Journal of Bioethical Inquiry,* 25 August 2020.

[5] China officially claims 5,000 COVID-19 deaths.

public diplomacy out of its medical assistance while exploiting the opportunity to mention the United States in highly unflattering terms. Xinhua, New China News Agency, offered the following: *"Greed will guide vaccine development and other efforts in the United States; China will share with the rest of the world, but the United States will keep resources for itself."*[6]

Nowhere in *Unrestricted Warfare* do Colonels Qiao and Wang explicitly advocate the use of biological weapons in the course of a war, protracted or otherwise. By the same token, the use of biological weapons is neither proscribed nor condemned. Without stretching what was written or not written, Qiao and Wang clearly outline a "battlefield beyond a battlefield" and would prefer to face an enemy seriously weakened by disease. Beijing cannot have missed the U.S. Navy's temporary loss of its aircraft carrier *USS Theodore Roosevelt* due to nearly twelve hundred sailors contracting COVID-19.[7] The idea of covert Chinese use of biological weapons in advance of armed conflict cannot be dismissed.

DIVISION OVER VACCINATIONS

An especially critical area in which Russian and Chinese disinformation has played a role is in exacerbating the ongoing debate between Americans advocating vaccination and those informally known as anti-vaxxers—stoutly opposing vaccination, the wearing of masks in public, and social distancing. Their opposition is based on the alleged infringement of personal rights.

The COVID-19 crisis has been accompanied by an increase in the quantity of online misinformation, sparking an "infodemic" (Brennen et al., 2020; Kouzy et al., 2020; World Health Organization, 2020). Anecdotal reports of

---

[6] Xinhua, 15 November 2020, "Commentary: A Disease-Ridden U.S. Fails World in Anti-Virus Cooperation"

[7] In March 2020, the USS Theodore Roosevelt was effectively put out of action when 1,200 of its crew members contracted COVID-19, with the majority being evacuated to Guam for treatment. See U.S. Naval Institute News; 23 June 2020. https://news.usni.org › Aviation. "Timeline: Theodore Roosevelt COVID-19 Outbreak Investigation." The infection may have been contracted during a port visit in Vietnam.

harms arising from such fake news stories are widespread; for example, it has been argued that exposure to COVID-19 fake news may undermine guidelines on social distancing, or encourage readers to self-medicate with unsanctioned treatments (e.g., Bavel et al., 2020; O'Connor & Murphy, 2020; Tasnim et al., 2020; Wright, 2020; Yoder, 2020)[8]

The FBI and Department of Homeland Security (DHS) have established the fact that Russia's Internet Research Agency seeded messages into American social media directed at both sides of this divisive issue. The Russian objective is to sow discord, but an important secondary benefit is to slow American measures aimed at curbing the virus. The spread of coronavirus in America is to Russia's advantage as it seeks political and territorial gains in Europe. An America weakened by disease is less capable of opposing Russian moves.

Campaigns against public health initiatives have been reported in a variety of countries. A case in point is Pakistan, where Islamic fundamentalist clerics concluded Islamic law was violated through forced vaccinations. Urged on by the disinformation from extremely conservative mullahs, mobs of angry Muslims beat nurses and health care workers sent by the government to vaccinate children against chronic diseases.

Though not physically violent, similar resistance to all vaccinations is taking place in the United States.

Widespread disinformation campaigns can also have demonstrable effects on health behaviors; for example, a drop in the rates of childhood vaccination against measles, mumps, and rubella has been directly tied to debunked misinformation linking the measles, mumps and rubella (MMR) vaccine with autism diagnoses (Leask et al., 2010).[9]

---

[8] C.M. Green and G. Murphy; "Quantifying the Effects of Fake News on Behavior: Evidence from a Study of COVID-19 Misinformation; Journal of Experimental Psychology: Applied, 10 June 2021

[9] Ibid.

The Chinese have cleverly aligned themselves with the political Rightwing and floated messages that vaccines infringe on American liberties. Messages directed to QAnon and other groups stress the "threat to freedom" from mandatory vaccines and masks. Rightwing extremists eagerly endorse the theme, unaware of Beijing's approval.

The issue of vaccination is an example of how Chinese and Russian covert influences have further polarized the American people. Messages from foreign sources posted on social media encourage Americans to assert their right to refuse vaccination. For example, one social media post shows the yellow flag of the coiled snake, traditionally from the Revolutionary War, with the words "Don't Jab on Me" superimposed on it.

A great percentage of individuals predisposed against government mandates uncritically accepted anti-vax social media messages and spread them.[10] While most such posts are from domestic sources, Moscow and Beijing have added numerous quiet endorsements— enough to keep the American discussion moving in their preferred direction. The result of the covert foreign anti-vaxxer campaign is to increase the COVID-19 infection rate and deaths while stirring enmity between Americans favoring vaccination and those opposed.

With millions infected, and nearly 900,000 deaths, COVID has had a huge negative social, economic, and political impact in the United States. It may take years for economic and social dislocation from this issue to resolve. The further spread of COVID-19 in the United States benefits no one—except our two adversaries, Russia and China.

Subtle and insubstantial, the expert leaves no trace;
divinely mysterious, he is inaudible. Thus he is master of his enemy's fate.

Sun Tzu

---

[10] NPR Morning edition, 5 December 2021, "Pro-Trump counties now have far higher death rates. Misinformation is to blame." www.npr.org/sections/health-shots/2021/12/05/1059828993/data-vaccine-misinformation-trump-counties-covid-death-rate

CHAPTER 14

A BIZARRE FRONT GROUP

*Seen in this perspective, action is the result of a certain number of
coordinated influences created by propaganda. Propaganda can make
the individual feel the urgency, the necessity, of some action, its unique
character. And at the same time propaganda shows him what to do. The
individual who burns with desire for action but does not know what to do
is a common type in our society. He wants to act for the sake of justice, peace,
progress, but does not know how. If propaganda can show him this "how," it
has won the game: action will surely follow.* [1]

Jacques Ellul

One innovation of the 1920s Cheka was the use of front groups.
Front groups are organizations that have no overt connection with the
Communist Party or any Russian entities. Front groups were called
upon to aid, or at least support, Soviet policies and initiatives. Some
front groups like the World Peace Council, the World Federation of
Trade Unions (WFTU), and The World Federation of Democratic
Youth, have been in existence for decades. These groups serve the dual
purpose of helping SVR case officers to spot and assess foreigners
who might be recruited as agents, and they serve as platforms for
the spread of print, electronic, and direct propaganda.[2] Today, most
of these front groups are known for what they are.

One of the most successful Russian deception operations in
history has been the manipulation—and *possibly even the creation*—
of a dangerous political movement in the U.S. known as QAnon.
Since its appearance in late 2017, QAnon has evolved into a shadowy
organization of extreme fanatics.

---

[1] Jacques Ellul, Propaganda: the Formation of Men's Attitudes, p. 209

[2] "Direct" propaganda includes speeches, seminars, marches, rallies, and other "propaganda of the deed."

The exact size of QAnon in America is unknown, but it is substantial.[3] A poll cited in the New York Times indicated that 15% of the American people either were members or fully accepted the beliefs of the QAnon movement.[4] Another segment of the American people accepts some, but not all, of QAnon's beliefs. QAnon membership varies by region and state and has spread from North America to Europe and Australia.

> Those who expressed belief in QAnon's premises were also far more likely than others to say they believe in other conspiracy theories, the poll found. Four in 10 said they thought that "the Covid-19 vaccine contains a surveillance microchip that is the sign of the beast in biblical prophecy."[5]

It should be mentioned that QAnon has its social roots in less educated, less sophisticated individuals who hold very fixed beliefs, and who, for one reason or another, are angry with the government as they perceive it to be. To that extent, the QAnon movement is a domestic, fundamentally populist movement with no particular ideology. Populist movements lend themselves to charismatic leaders who present themselves as the solution to the movement's perceived grievances.[6]

QAnon came into existence through an anonymous Internet posting by a figure identifying himself only as "Q." The identity of Q has never been revealed, and Q may not even exist as a real human being. Although the bizarre movement may be homegrown, we will not know for sure until Q is eventually proved to be an American

---

[3] QAnon has since expanded to Europe, Canada, Japan, Latin America and Australia. Its views are profoundly anti-democratic, conspiratorial, and sensational. Its goal is to divide and to agitate groups to action.

[4] New York Times, "QAnon Now as Popular in U.S. as Some Major Religions, Poll Suggests," 12 August 2021

[5] NYT, op.cit.

[6] Latin American Communists, in particular the Nicaraguan Sandinistas, have for long made use of organizations and individuals unaffiliated with the Party or its leaders. These people and groups are called "Tontos utiles," which translates as "Useful fools." The name is appropriately applied to QAnon members.

citizen. *Regardless, there is no question that QAnon received extensive prompting from Russian sources for nearly 39 months.*

Due to Russian manipulation and because of its avowedly anti-American subversive nature, QAnon may be considered a Russian front group. The person or group behind Q presented a contorted view of lies and distortions to a carefully chosen target audience in the United States. QAnon describes a vast conspiracy surrounding the U.S. government and key political figures. This supposed Washington cabal caught the attention of extreme conspiracy theorists and militants.

Although speculative, the possibility cannot be ruled out that perhaps Q is a tech-savvy young Russian case officer or group of Russian trolls that have in-depth computer operations expertise.[7] If so, the QAnon movement in the West was the result of a well-crafted Russian false flag operation. In the best tradition of the Cheka, a false flag is designed to attract and manipulate people holding extremist political views.

False flag operations are difficult to undertake and extremely delicate, even for gifted case officers. In the past, Russian intelligence officers have convincingly assumed identities as varied as Tsarist officers, German Nazis, or Turkish Grey Wolves, depending on the perceived operational need. It is not too much of a stretch to believe a talented young Russian case officer is Q. Like an internet Pied Piper, Q has led a collection of American yokels and fanatics on a long journey to nowhere.

Q's first posting appeared on the "4chan" anonymous message board in October 2017. After that, Q began to weave a convoluted plot involving a supposed deep state opposed to Donald J. Trump. The deep state was said to be run by cannibals, pedophiles, and sex traffickers associated with prominent Democrats such as Barack Obama and Hilary Clinton. QAnon believes a group of American Satanists planned to unseat then-President Trump, but that Trump—with QAnon's assistance—would stage a preemptive countercoup

---

[7] This may initially have been a Russian "troll" operation -- since December 2020 assumed by the Chinese.

on a secret date, called "Storm." The goal of the counter-coup would be to restore America's rightful ruler, Trump.

According to the wild conspiracy views projected by QAnon, Trump intended to carry out mass arrests of the Satanist plotters. With that end in view, Trump faked Russian meddling in the 2016 Election as a means of identifying and trapping his foes.

The great majority of the rioters who stormed the Capitol Building January 6, 2021, were QAnon members or sympathizers. QAnon and allied groups were poised to launch a coup well prior to January 6, as investigative journalism has shown.

> Within days of President Donald Trump's election defeat, Stewart Rhodes began talking about the Insurrection Act as critical to the country's future.

> The bombastic founder of the extremist group Oath Keepers told followers that the obscure, rarely used law would allow Trump to declare a national emergency so dire that the military, militias or both would be called out to keep him in the White House.

> Appearing Nov. 9, 2020, as a guest on the InfoWars program of conspiracy theorist Alex Jones, Rhodes urged Trump to invoke the act "to suppress the deep state" and claimed Oath Keepers already had men "stationed outside D.C. as a nuclear option."[8]

Had the Insurrection Act been involved—essentially triggering a *coup d'etat*—the Russians could not have been more pleased. Indeed, their greatest hopes would have been realized in such a coup. The ensuing political and social chaos would have paralyzed America, thereby rendering the U.S. incapable of interfering in Russian military

---

[8] Devlin Barrett and Spencer S. Hsu, "Insurrection," Washington Post, 23 January 2022

moves in eastern Europe or the Middle East. *Active measures would therefore have accomplished what Russian tanks and artillery could not.*[9]

Press reporting has amply covered the rioting on January 6, 2021, which resulted in the storming of the Capitol and the deaths of five people. While it is not possible to determine which country and which set of messages helped trigger the rioting, it can be said that China and Russia certainly contributed to the mayhem. The great majority of the rioters were members and followers of QAnon. As noted by Cohen, China surpassed Russia as the "primary foreign actor" posting QAnon-related narratives touting "deep states" and cabals of various kinds to extremist minds.

PROOF OF ENEMY INFLUENCE

The timing of Q's appearance in October 2017 may not be coincidental. Department of Homeland Security officials reported that in June 2017, *"individuals linked to the Kremlin attempted to infiltrate election-related computer systems in more than twenty U.S. states. Authorities believe that whilst the Russian hackers did not tamper with the vote count, they were probing election systems for vulnerabilities."*[10]

Reuters reported that a team of researchers from the Pew Research Group reviewed an extensive archive of online postings connected with the QAnon deception and disinformation operation. Their findings revealed a pattern of a gradual fostering of the movement.

A more granular review by Reuters shows Russian accounts began amplifying the movement as it started, early in the previous month. [ed. October 2017]

---

[9] It must be borne in mind that although Russia's economy is less than one fifth that of China, and thus poses a minimal economic threat to the United States, its military power remains formidable. Vladimir Putin has made no secret of his desire to rebuild the power and territory of the former Soviet Union which he once served proudly. To achieve that goal Putin must keep the U.S. off balance. The best way to do this is to foment internal disorder and confusion throughout American society.

[10] DHS, op.cit., p. 28

From November 2017 on, QAnon was the single most frequent hashtag tweeted by accounts that Twitter has since identified as Russian-backed, a Reuters analysis of the archive shows, with the term used some 17,000 times.

The archives contain more than 4,000 accounts that Twitter suspended for spreading Russian government disinformation in 2018 and 2019 but preserved for researchers.[11]

The QAnon deception operation was given a strong boost by Rightwing extremist and unwitting Russian collaborator, Tracy Diaz, a key spokesperson.[12] She often posted online materials promoting QAnon's themes, and Reuters notes she presently has over 10 million views on YouTube.

"The trove shows that some of the Russian accounts tweeted about QAnon's most important popularizer [ed. Ms. Diaz] even before the anonymous figure known as Q emerged, then rewarded her with more promotion when she put videos about Q on YouTube."[13] Why not promote her? After all, Ms. Diaz was doing superb work for the SVR and GRU.

CNN reported that in early 2021 China may have surpassed Russia in its covert influence via QAnon. The last identified Russian Q posting was made in December 2020. According to the FBI, since late 2020, China, Iran, and even Saudi Arabia have picked up the task of shepherding the QAnon movement's membership from the Russians. CNN's Zachary Cohen, reporting in April 2021, noted the following:

"In both 2020 and for the first two months of 2021, almost one-fifth of all QAnon posts on Facebook originated from administrators overseas," the report states.

---

[11] Joseph Menn, "QAnon received earlier boost from Russian accounts on Twitter, archives show;" Reuters, 2 November 2020

[12] Joseph Menn, op.cit.

[13] Joseph Menn, op.cit.

> While the report found that Russian actors were behind the majority of this activity last year [ed. 2020], it says China emerged as "the primary foreign actor touting QAnon-narratives online" in 2021, timing that coincides with Beijing's ramp up of disinformation efforts targeting the US more broadly.[14]

The question arises about how much coordination is taking place between Beijing and Moscow in manipulating the QAnon masses. For the most part, foreign intelligence services prefer to work separately, but clearly, for both Russia and China, the United States is a common target. Since the goals of Beijing and Moscow are quite similar regarding America, cooperation between Chinese and Russian intelligence services regarding QAnon is entirely plausible.

From the Chinese perspective, encouraging the growth of QAnon—and the spread of violence in the U.S.—suits their policies perfectly. QAnon violence not only hampers American interference with China's overseas ambitions but can be played to China's domestic audience as an example of what American democracy is really like.

As previously discussed, China makes excellent use of foreign intellectuals, milking them for their research, knowledge, and professional contacts. While there is far more to gain from courting scientists and engineers than from minding fools, China nevertheless has found ways to make excellent use of America's many thousands of semi-educated fools. They do, however, require some careful shepherding. Piggybacking on the Russian troll operation, the Chinese were doing nothing more than capitalizing upon an already-successful divisive campaign in America's capital, at very little cost to themselves. *The Chinese clearly understand that even American fools have their uses.*

---

[14] Zachary Cohen, "China and Russia 'weaponized' QAnon conspiracy around time of US capital attack, report says," CNN; www.cnn.com/2021/04/19/politics/qanon-russia-china-amplification/index.html/

Whether or not the Russians originated the QAnon operation, they have masterfully manipulated it. True, it did ultimately "fail" if its purpose was to ensure the reelection of Donald J. Trump in November 2020. Yet, QAnon made great headway toward a more important Russian goal: creating and directing a powerful, destructive Trojan Horse inside Russia's main enemy, the United States. QAnon is still very much alive and, whether directed by Chinese or Russian masters, will continue to play a destructive part in American political life.

There is nothing more frightening than ignorance in action.[15]

Johann Wolfgang von Goethe

---

[15] Goethe lived 1749-1832.

CLOSING THOUGHTS

*The only thing necessary for the triumph of evil
is for good men to do nothing.*

Edmund Burke[1]

In the preceding chapters, we have glimpsed some of the means
the Russian Federation and the People's Republic of China have used
to divide the American people, weaken our nation, and ultimately
eliminate our values from shaping the global future.

We have reviewed the historical and cultural roots of Russian
and Chinese hostility and the reasons motivating them to conduct a
relentless, silent war on the West and its friends. In a sense, none of
this is new. Russia's use of propaganda, front groups, Fifth Column
movements, and constant pressure dates to Cheka times in the 1920s.
For the People's Republic of China, the offensive against the West
is more recent. What is new is Russia's and China's unparalleled
ability to disinform, mislead, and divide the American public thanks
to technology.

We have examined current Chinese political-military doctrine,
which in some respects is ancient, yet is also ultra-modern and
profound. While Russian military-political thinking appears to lag
that of China, Moscow's operational ability to find cracks and weak
spots in Western societies is well-honed. We have seen how Moscow
helped foster an all-American gang of QAnon stooges to disrupt
Constitutional procedures. The Russians also used hacking and
clever planting of stolen information to influence national elections.

We have surveyed how effectively Russian intelligence services
hacked the files of the Democratic National Committee, how they
hacked into our economic infrastructure, and how they fostered a
brigade of feather-brained loud-mouthed "useful idiots" ranging
from Alex Jones to the QAnon mob.

---

[1] English political philosopher, who lived 1729-1797.

It is a foregone conclusion that the Russians will persist in their disinformation aimed at dividing the American people. It is also certain that they will continue to steal whatever they can. We may safely surmise that the Russian intelligence services are emplacing "sleeper bots" and other cyber mines into pipelines, communications networks, water supplies, electrical power systems, and literally any critical American asset they can hack. To make matters worse, they will mobilize front groups to wreak havoc when their need is greatest.

Journalists and scholars have documented bits and pieces of Sino-Russian efforts to destabilize the West. This book was an attempt to show how all the reported pieces come together like a mosaic. Some pieces are brightly colored and obvious; other pieces are subtle, often overlooked, or not even visible. Taken together, all of the pieces constitute a protracted, persistent strategy that has one goal: destabilizing the United States from within.

This book has not made an attempt to prescribe specific measures for dealing with the invisible war in which we are unwillingly engaged. That is left for others to decide, not only specialists in the cyber security community but especially our fellow citizens and elected representatives—while we still have them.

It is recommended for thoughtful citizens and moderate political leaders to take heed of the warnings in this book, and decide upon appropriate measures while there is still time.

Forewarned is forearmed.
Miguel de Cervantes[2]

---

[2] Spain's greatest writer, who lived 1547-1616

ABOUT THE AUTHOR

COLONEL G.L. LAMBORN

G.L. Lamborn is a retired U.S. Army Reserve full Colonel and CIA Senior Operations Officer with more than forty years (1967-2013) of service to the American people. His duty stations included Vietnam, Korea, Iraq, Afghanistan, El Salvador, and many other Third World hot spots. He is a specialist in insurgency and revolutionary warfare and the author of *Arms of Little Value* (Casemate, 2012), *Jihad of the Pen* (DIA, 2010), *The People in Arms* (DIA, 2009), and co-author of *To Blind the Eyes of Our Enemies* (White Hart Publications, 2018).

Larry holds a B.A. in History from Washington University in St. Louis, an M.A. in Chinese Studies from the University of Washington in Seattle, and is an Air War College graduate.

A Life Member of the American Legion and Past Commander of Post 177 in Fairfax, Virginia, Larry continued to serve his neighbors as president of the North Central Thousand Oaks Neighborhood Association (2013-2020) and is now on the City of San Antonio Redistricting Advisory Committee.

CPSIA information can be obtained
at www.ICGtesting.com
Printed in the USA
BVHW071210090822
644143BV00012B/1302